DON'T
CALL IT
LOVE

DON'T CALL IT LOVE

Breaking the Cycle
of Relationship Dependency

DR. GREGORY L. JANTZ
and DR. TIM CLINTON
with Ann McMurray

Revell
a division of Baker Publishing Group
Grand Rapids, Michigan

© 2015 by Dr. Gregory L. Jantz and Dr. Tim Clinton

Published by Revell
a division of Baker Publishing Group
P.O. Box 6287, Grand Rapids, MI 49516-6287
www.revellbooks.com

Printed in the United States of America

Library of Congress Cataloging-in-Publication Data
Jantz, Gregory L.
    Don't call it love : breaking the cycle of relationship dependency / Dr.
  Gregory L. Jantz and Dr. Tim Clinton, with Ann McMurray.
      pages cm
    Includes bibliographical references.
    ISBN 978-0-8007-2675-1 (pbk.)
    1. Relationship addiction—Religious aspects—Christianity.
  2. Codependency—Religious aspects—Christianity. 3. Interpersonal
  relations—Religious aspects—Christianity. I. Title.
  BV4596.R43J36 2015
  248.4—dc23   2015018607

Unless otherwise indicated, Scripture quotations are from the Holy Bible, New International Version®. NIV®. Copyright © 1973, 1978, 1984, 2011 by Biblica, Inc.™ Used by permission of Zondervan. All rights reserved worldwide. www.zondervan.com

Scripture quotations labeled NIV 1984 are from the Holy Bible, New International Version®. NIV®. Copyright © 1973, 1978, 1984 by Biblica, Inc.™ Used by permission of Zondervan. All rights reserved worldwide. www.zondervan.com

18   19   20   21   7   6   5   4   3

green
press
INITIATIVE

We dedicate this book
to those struggling with dependency
who know there's more to relationships
than what they've experienced,
who refuse to stop until they find a better way.

Contents

Acknowledgment

Both of us would like to acknowledge the work of Lonnie Hull DuPont, executive editor at Revell, for her insightful and invaluable contributions.

Introduction

What Is Relationship Dependency?

Having coauthors on a book about relationships seems fitting. The two of us (Dr. Gregg and Dr. Tim) have known each other professionally and personally for years. We have presented information together at annual conferences and through webinars for the American Association of Christian Counselors. We've gotten to know and trust each other. In our professional lives, each of us has counseled people who experience difficulty in their relationships. These are people who are drawn to relationships, but those relationships are a source of continual struggle and stress.

Where would we be without relationships? The short answer to that question is we would be alone. While alone can feel good for some, alone does not always feel good for most. We look to relationships to help us frame our lives, to give us identity and purpose. We rely on relationships for affirmation and affection. When our circumstances change—locations, jobs, health—relationships can be the glue that holds the rest of our lives together.

Our relationships are supposed to give us love, strength, encouragement, and affirmation. Our relationships are supposed to tie us to others in positive and uplifting ways. Sadly, some do not. Why and how do some relationships create heartache and havoc? Why and how do some relationships bring desperation, frustration, and unmet needs? Why and how do some relationships that should produce comfort produce pain instead?

There are so many questions concerning relationships. How do you know what the relationship rules are? How do you know when you're offtrack in a relationship? When is doing too much really doing too much? When are the expectations of the other person unreasonable? When are your own expectations unreasonable? How can you say no without risk? If relationships are supposed to be about give-and-take, why do some relationships seem so one-sided? How can you avoid a backlash of struggle, frustration, and unmet expectations?

The answers to questions such as these are complex because relationships are complex. No check-off-the-box propositions, relationships are an amalgamation of needs, a meshing of expectations, and a breeding ground for both positive and negative emotions. Relationships help you establish bonds with other people while affecting the bond you have with yourself. On the surface, relationships are about other people, but ultimately, your relationships say a great deal about *you*. Relationships are windows of the soul, reflecting your inner needs and deeply held beliefs. Any relationship you have with another person reveals how you feel about yourself.

For some people, relationships become a minefield of frustration and dissatisfaction. These relationships don't seem to get better but languish in a perpetual place of pain. As difficult as a relationship seems, the thought of being without the relationship is worse. Within this tension of can't-live-with and can't-live-without lies relationship dependency. Relationship dependency happens when a person becomes dependent on relationships to function in life.

At the core, a person who is dependent on relationships has difficulty loving or trusting self and needs relationships to provide validation and value. When a dependent person seeks identity, safety, and meaning in life through another person, staying with that person becomes a matter of survival. Ask why someone who is physically abused would stay in that relationship, and relationship dependency becomes an answer. Ask why someone would allow being verbally or emotionally battered day after day, and relationship dependency becomes an answer. Ask why someone always seems to jump from one intense relationship to another, and relationship dependency becomes an answer. Relationship dependency creates situations in which the other person becomes the air the dependent person breathes, their very means of survival.

Relationship dependent people will often put up with the terrible because the alternative—being alone—is unthinkable. Dependent people may come to resent and distrust the other person in the relationship, but they resent and distrust themselves more. When you've lived your life within dependent relationships, it can be difficult to realize something is wrong because life seems normal. And even when you realize something is wrong, the relationship can feel safer than the alternative—to be alone and without the relationship.

Any relationship starts with two people. However, overcoming relationship dependency starts not with the other person but with you. Becoming aware of yourself, your attitudes, your behaviors, and how you react and respond to others is vital to creating healthy relationships. Know yourself first, have a strong and healthy relationship with yourself first, and then you can move on to strong and healthy relationships with others.

Our goal is to guide you through a discovery of how patterns of dependency may be playing out within your relationships. One of the ways we'll do this is through the Connection Points found in each chapter. These Connection Points are opportunities for you to write, reflect, and challenge yourself toward deeper understanding, to bring you closer to recovery. Learning where you are doesn't mean you have to stay there. Learning where you are is the first step in moving somewhere else. Understanding where you are and moving toward where you want to be require you to do the following:

- You must look at the *pattern* of your relationships, not just the aspects of a *single* relationship.
- You must realize the key person in relationship dependency is not the *other person*; the key person in relationship dependency is *you*.

You can fill up your world with the sights, sounds, and concerns of other people. You can spend your waking hours focused on the needs of others and spend your sleepless nights terrified over your own needs. You can watch your life become a revolving door of broken, unsatisfying relationships. Or you can take a journey of discovery toward understanding how to free yourself from patterns of the past and create healthy relationships going forward.

If you're tired of where you are, take the journey.

If you've realized there simply has to be more to relationships than what you've experienced, take the journey.

If you're beginning to recognize negative relationship patterns but have no idea how to stop them, take the journey.

Once you start the journey, keep your eyes open as much as possible, guard your heart as little as possible, and withhold immediate judgment and allow time for understanding to soak in and permeate dried, damaged places.

Change is hard but not as hard as staying stuck. The only way to get unstuck is to move.

1

Why the Key
to Relationships Is You

The house was too quiet; it was always too quiet whenever the kids were gone. The thought of only herself for company was a familiar terror. She couldn't really blame the kids; she wasn't good company. In desperation, she flung open the cabinet and decided to bake cookies. When the kids got home, the smell would entice them into the kitchen, and maybe they'd stay. If they didn't, the cookies would still be there.

Do you ever feel that way? Terrified of being alone? Worried alone is how you'll end up? Worried that the people you love will abandon you? This fear of being alone, abandoned, and rejected is a familiar fear for those who find themselves dependent on relationships. The pain of that fear creates a tremendous motivation to be in and stay in relationships. Clinging to relationships, then, is the symptom of dependency, but the cause is fear—fear of being alone, fear of self.

■ The Heart of Relationship Dependency Is Fear

How do you talk to yourself? When something bad happens, do you jump in to take the blame? When something good happens, are you the last to claim credit? What sort of reasons do you give for the things that happen to you and around you? How quick are you to forgive yourself when you mess up? Do you expect yourself to mess up?

What do you do when you are your own worst enemy? How do you get away from yourself when you take yourself everywhere you go? How do you escape from that constant condemning, criticizing, or demeaning voice when it's the voice inside your head? Where can you run when the thing you fear most is yourself?

When people fear themselves, they will sometimes turn to activities to try to outrun the fear. They may use alcohol, drugs, shopping, eating, gambling, or the internet to keep from being alone with themselves. Other people may turn to family, friends, co-workers, anyone to crowd out their fear of being alone. For those who turn to people, relationships, in a sense, become their drug of choice, the way they cope with their fear of being alone.

Relationships were not meant to be based on fear. Relationships were meant to provide stability, strength, and a launching point for independence in life. Relationships were meant to provide a place to grow up, launch out, and come into your own. Something in that process gets twisted in relationship dependency. Instead of providing and enhancing independence, relationships become an avenue for dependence.

At the heart of relationship dependency is fear, the fear that the dependent person is not enough. This realization that "I am not enough" is, in a sense, true. We were made for relationships and were not meant to exist as lone rangers in the world. But for a dependent person, the understanding that "I am not enough" is followed with a judgment of "Therefore, I am flawed and unlovable."

If you believe you are flawed and unlovable, this harsh judgment can undermine your relationships. You may reach out to others seeking completeness but remain fearful of being unworthy of those relationships. Those relationships become vital for your sense of security, but that sense of security is never fully realized: "I am not enough, so I seek out others, but I am unworthy to be loved by others."

Your Relationship with Yourself

How you feel about yourself affects all of your other relationships. Some of you may not be used to the idea that you have a distinct relationship with yourself, but you do. You have a personality and a will; you have a perspective on life that is lived out in how you think, speak, feel, and act. Every day you interact with yourself; you carry on conversations with yourself, verbal or otherwise; you make judgments about yourself and see life from the prism of your own worldview. You are a force in your world, whether you choose to acknowledge it or not.

You have a relationship with yourself, and how you view that relationship matters. Some people will understand this relationship with self from a positive position in which self is acknowledged and appreciated. This positive identity is internalized and accepted: "I like myself," "I forgive myself," "I understand myself."

Others will understand this relationship with self from a negative position, sometimes distancing from self through the use of second person: "Why did *you* do that?" "How can *you* be so stupid?" "When will *you* ever learn?" For these people, self is not a source of strength and comfort but a source of concern and fear. When self is the enemy, each day is a battlefield and involves fighting with self, trying to be with self as little as possible, finding ways to distract and create distance from self.

How do you refer to yourself? When you do something you think is wrong, what do you tell yourself? Do you accuse yourself with statements such as "What were you thinking?" and "How could you let that happen?" When you do something wrong, do you still like yourself? Can you forgive yourself? When you do something right, are you able to acknowledge yourself?

When your relationship with self is rife with conflict, your relationships with others often mirror that turmoil. If you're afraid to really know who you are, how can you give yourself to others? If you don't love who you are, how can you truly love other people? If you don't like yourself, how can you expect others to like you? If you don't trust yourself, how can you ever learn to trust anyone else?

When your relationship with self is suspect, your relationships with others become suspect. When your relationships with others become suspect, those relationships have shaky foundations. The shakier those relationships are, the more time, energy, and effort need to be placed into shoring them up and attempting to control them. The more those relationships are controlled, the more prone they are to disappoint. The more those relationships disappoint, the greater the need to replace them with new relationships. This is the cycle of relationship dependency and why it is not enough to try to fix the other person or to find the "right" person. The relationship that must be repaired first is with self.

When You Are Not Enough

As we said before, a dependent person has a variety of ways to fill the voids they feel. While they may choose a *something* to hold off the terror of self, they will also often choose a *someone*. When a dependent person chooses a *someone* to fill the void, they create relationship dependency. Through their relationships, they cry out, "I am unable to love myself, so you must love me for me."

Choosing a *someone* when you don't feel worthy of that relationship in the first place is precarious; that relationship is built on a shaky foundation. What do you do with a shaky foundation? You try to shore it up. You hem that foundation in on all sides with concrete. You construct a wooden box around it. You bind steel into its parts so it cannot move. While all of this shoring and hemming and binding may work well with buildings, these methods are less successful with people, who require a certain amount of flexibility in relationships. A building may need to stay in the same spot for a hundred years, but relationships never do.

Relationships do best when there is room to move as people change and grow. If you are dependent on a relationship, however, you may be terrified of that relationship changing and growing. How do you know that change and growth won't result in the loss of the relationship? With such fear, you may determine you are safer and more secure with a

21

relationship that stays the same. So you go about shoring up and hemming in the relationship, as much as you are able, so it can't move. This rigidity puts tremendous pressure on a relationship that is already inherently unstable. Why is the relationship inherently unstable? Because its foundation is based on a damaged relationship with self.

Who would enter into such a shaky relationship? Sometimes a dependent person will seek out a relationship with a person who has an appropriate sense of self. A so-called normal or healthy person can be attractive to a dependent person. A dependent person becomes quite adept at modifying their behaviors, especially in the beginning of a relationship, a relationship they believe they need to function. However, over time, the healthy person may become aware that there is something shaky about the relationship. Words such as *clingy*, *suffocating*, or *controlling* may be used to describe the relationship. The healthy person might comment that the other person seemed so charming, nice, and accommodating at first but later became demanding, manipulative, and overly emotional. When the dysfunction of the relationship becomes too extreme, the so-called normal person will often end the relationship.

If so-called normal people resist staying in a dependent relationship, who is left? Sometimes two dependent people will enter into a relationship, but these are extremely shaky relationships because neither person feels competent or capable to provide direction for the other or the relationship. This leaves dependent people vulnerable to another personality type. They can be susceptible to people with arrogant and narcissistic personality types who believe they always know the right answer. Certain types of people will seek out a dependent personality because of their need for power and control. The dependent person cries out, "Please, tell me what to do!" and the abusive or arrogant or narcissistic person is all too willing to do just that in every situation.

There are also people who seek out a dependent personality because they need someone to support and enable their lifestyle. An alcoholic or a drug addict needs people who will contribute to and enable the addiction and not ask questions or object. People who are addicted to their own power and control over others will seek out a relationship with a person who doesn't trust himself or herself. People who need compliance for behaviors will seek out people who need to comply. This is the nature of codependency.

Because dependent and codependent relationships are dysfunctional, they carry the seeds of their own destruction. These relationships can limp along, sometimes for years, under stress, requiring large amounts of effort and energy to maintain before they finally fall apart. When they do, the dependent person can be left feeling betrayed, abandoned, vulnerable, and desperate to find a new relationship to latch on to for safety. In that desperation, the dependent person may be even more vulnerable to another dysfunctional and potentially abusive relationship.

The consequences of relationship dependency can be as devastating to relationships as alcoholism, drug abuse, chronic gambling, or other behaviors that erode the foundation of family and friendship. When patterns of behavior are so deeply embedded into who you are, how you were raised, and how you view life, how can you come to recognize the truth? If you are already seeing the pain and problems within your relationships, you are beginning to see the truth.

▉ Connection Point

Write your name at the top of a piece of paper. Then number the left-hand side of the paper from 1 to 10. Write down words or phrases you believe describe who you are. Some of you may be able to come up with ten personal descriptions immediately. Others of you may require more time. Give yourself the time to come up with no less than ten.

Next to each word or phrase you've written, indicate with either a plus or a minus sign whether the word or phrase—as it applies to you—is a positive or a negative. (For example, one person might write "detail-oriented" and mean that as a positive, that they are able to track multiple details at once. Another person might write "detail-oriented" and mean that as a negative, as nitpicky and requiring rigid order.) Then answer the following questions:

1. How difficult was it for you to come up with ten words?
2. Which would have been harder for you—coming up with ten positive words or coming up with ten negative words?
3. How many of your ten are negative, and how many are positive?
4. Are positives and negatives evenly dispersed throughout your list, or does one category come first?
5. If one category comes first, which one—positive or negative?

People who do not like or trust themselves will tend to focus on negatives when doing self-evaluations. If asked to list personal flaws, they are readily able to do so. If asked to list personal strengths, they often have difficulty doing so. When they are able to come up with a positive, they may qualify that positive by adding that this trait is not as strong in themselves as in other people they know or find another way to devalue it. Some dependent people are unable to come up with a positive word to say about themselves and will simply leave their paper blank.

Over the years, we have been surprised by the number of people who struggle to view themselves in a positive light. Unable to give themselves validation and approval, these individuals are susceptible to giving undue weight to the influence and presence of others. This first Connection Point is a way for you to understand how you view yourself—positively or negatively. Again, understanding a starting point doesn't mean you have to stay there. Your journey from negative to positive is just beginning.

2

How Do You Know You Are Dependent?

There is a temptation in relationship dependency to focus on the relationship side of the equation. But the key to knowing how susceptible you are to relationship dependency is to focus on the dependency side of the equation. You need to ask yourself, "Do I have a dependent personality, or do I tend to display dependent personality traits?" If you are a person who displays dependency traits, then it is likely those dependency traits will show up in your relationships.

Following are traits associated with a dependent personality. These traits are not always easy to read and identify with; we understand that. We understand and appreciate how difficult it is for people to look so deeply in the mirror. As therapists who have worked with and seen the amazing benefits of recovery, we also understand and appreciate how vital such a deep look is to healing and growth.

Because we have worked with others on dependency issues, we know that each person will come to a crossroads where they must decide to continue down the challenging path of self-discovery. Those who find themselves dependent—whether on alcohol or drugs, food, gambling, shopping, or relationships—will come to that crossroads. Our hope is that you will continue down your path with the same courage and determination we've seen lead others to healing and recovery.

Dependent Personality Traits

Those who are dependent often have the following personality traits.

They have difficulty making everyday decisions without advice and reassurance.

The key here is *everyday decisions*. If you're going to make a major purchase or engage in a major life change, of course you would talk over your decision and get opinions from friends and family, even experts. But a dependent personality faces everyday, almost trivial, decisions from a position of hesitation and fear.

For example, say you are sent to the store to buy a loaf of bread. For a dependent person, the difficulty is not buying bread; the difficulty is buying the *wrong* bread. The difficulty is taking the wrong street or choosing the wrong brand or paying the wrong price. The difficulty is the terror of being *wrong*. People with dependent personalities distrust their ability to make right choices and have great difficulty forgiving themselves when they make a wrong one. Decisions, then, become *mind*-fields, with potentially disastrous results. To avoid making the wrong choice, dependent people will avoid making decisions on their own. They will seek out advice and direction from others and, even after the decision is made, will continue to seek reassurance they've made the right choice.

They need others to assume responsibility for many major areas of life.

Asking for help from another person in a major area of life is one thing. Expecting that other person to take over responsibility for you is another. People with dependent personalities give up control of major areas of life to another person out of fear. Life challenges can take on the dimensions of insurmountable difficulties and are, therefore, seen as impossible to deal with alone. Life challenges, though, are the ways each of us is stretched and grows. We learn from our mistakes and victories and mature into healthier, happier people. When you are dependent on others to solve the puzzles of life for you, you are robbed of these incredible opportunities for personal growth.

They have difficulty disagreeing with others out of fear.

Have you ever seen that tongue-in-cheek sign that says, "Everyone is entitled to their own opinion, as long as it agrees with mine?" A dependent person has a variation on that sign: "I am entitled to my own opinion, as long as it agrees with yours." Both of these signs are saying the same thing: You are not entitled to your own opinion. A dependent person does not feel worthy to express or have an opinion that differs from someone they feel they need. That person could be a boss, a spouse, a parent, a child, a friend—just about anyone the dependent person is in a relationship with. Dependent people are terrified of being *wrong*, but they are also terrified of being *right*, if that right brings them into conflict with someone they depend on. Tragically, in dependency, truth becomes secondary.

Everyone is entitled to their own opinion. Those opinions are what brings diversity, complexity, and texture to human relationships. Those opinions are also what helps others to contemplate a different point of view and may allow a hidden truth to be revealed. Refusing to consider a truth you might not know is denying yourself. Overlooking a truth you do know is also denying yourself.

They struggle to start projects or do things on their own.

Dependent people fear exposure. They fear exposure because exposure may cause others to realize how "worthless" they really are. They fear having their failures and weaknesses on public display. One way dependent people avoid failure is to avoid taking the initiative. They don't put themselves out in front of others by taking the initiative or promising results. Taking the initiative is ripe for risk of failure and therefore is to be avoided. If you believe you are doomed to fail at a task, you are not motivated to engage in that task; you are motivated to avoid the task.

This fear-based life does not produce growth. Think about babies. If risk was to be avoided at all costs, babies would never become toddlers. To toddle means to walk with short, unsteady steps. Walking with short, unsteady steps is risky. You could trip; you could fall. Babies who lie around on a blanket are safe, while toddlers have to contend with dangerous things like table edges and stairs. But who wants to remain a baby? Isn't the risk of a bonked head or a skinned knee worth the freedom in learning to walk? Dependent people often make decisions that will allow them to stay on the blanket.

To gain approval, they may do things they don't want to do.

Relationships shouldn't be about bribery, about what you've done for me lately. People with dependent personalities distrust themselves and, therefore, don't trust their relationships. As a way to control a shaky relationship, they may attempt to purchase the relationship. They may say yes to things they wouldn't ordinarily do in order to maintain the relationship, even things that may be frightening or damaging. Dependent people can give up much in order to maintain the relationship.

They feel anxious or distressed when alone or thinking about being alone.

Dependent people often expect the worst. They do not feel competent to live their own lives without others. Being alone means being unprotected by others and vulnerable. The thought of being alone to cope with whatever "worst" life throws at them is simply overwhelming. This sense of being overwhelmed leads to anxiety. If you have this dependency trait, your thoughts will race to the worst possibilities until those possibilities become near certainties. Dependent people wholeheartedly believe in Murphy's Law—anything that can go wrong will go wrong. If you are a dependent person, you will often find yourself believing in the inevitability of the worst happening and in your own failure to cope.

They urgently seek another relationship when a close relationship ends.

When a close relationship ends, for whatever reason, it should be a time for you to go over the positives and the negatives of that relationship and to consider any personal changes you want to make. When a close relationship ends, there is a natural time for healing, for reflection, and for personal growth. This is a time to reconnect with friends and family, with people who know and love you and can help you put the loss of the relationship into perspective. The end of a relationship is a time for reconnecting with yourself and rediscovering areas of personal interest. This is a time to get comfortable again in your own skin, without the covering of the other person.

Dependent people do not give themselves this kind of time for recovery. Instead, they are frantic for a new relationship. As soon as one relationship ends, they are desperate to find and engage in another. When you run from person to person, you are often not running *to* anyone; you are running *away* from yourself.

They feel better solving the problems of others.

One of the ways dependent people tie others to them is through filling needs. In this disconnected, don't-have-time society we live in, a listening ear is a valuable commodity. Some dependent people know this and are willing, even eager, to provide that listening ear, that shoulder to cry on. Dependent people want others to tell them their problems. By helping others, they are often helping themselves by distracting themselves from their own problems.

Dependent people can crave the attention and validation they receive when other people give them their trust. Lacking self-trust, dependent people can be tempted to live vicariously off the trust given to them by others. Dependent people can appear so sure of themselves, with all the right answers, at least all the right answers for other people's problems. Yet their lives and relationships don't bear the fruit of their own advice.

They put the needs of others above their own needs.

Dependent people become good at meeting the needs of others. They can become so good at meeting the needs of others that they have little time to attend to their own needs. This makes it difficult to maintain healthy boundaries in relationships. Healthy boundaries within relationships certainly allow for the needs of others but not to the exclusion of self needs. Healthy boundaries allow for one person to help another without becoming self-depleted. Those who set healthy boundaries understand you cannot continue to give to others when you have used up all of yourself.

Dependent people are fearful of setting too many boundaries because they are afraid those boundaries will cause the relationship to fail. Because dependent people feel they must have the relationship, they will do things they would not normally do and act in ways they would not normally act in order to maintain the relationship.

In some family relationships, one person may recognize this lack of boundaries and begin to use that dependency for personal advantage. That person can be a spouse, a sibling, a parent, or a child. These people may manipulate circumstances in order to force the dependent person to "prove" their love by catering to their needs. Having determined the dependent person is a giver in the relationship, this person will intentionally adopt the role of taker. The taker may inwardly despise the giver and assign the giver blame for their own taking behavior. The dependent person willingly accepts the blame as a way to maintain the relationship.

They take on responsibility for meeting hurtful, difficult, or even impossible needs.

When you have a dependent personality, you need others to give you companionship, affirmation, attention, or validation. In exchange, you may barter for those needs by trying to fulfill the needs of others, even if those needs are hurtful or unreasonable. You are afraid to say no because you're afraid you'll hear no back when it comes to staying in the relationship. You can become so focused on the harm you think you'll feel if you hear no that you blind yourself to the harm done by always saying yes. The harm done by always saying yes happens not only to you but also to the other person, who does not learn about healthy boundaries.

They make themselves responsible when bad things happen.

Life happens; things happen. Sometimes those things are bad things. Dependent people, who do not love or trust themselves, are quick to assign themselves blame for those bad things, even if that judgment is unreasonable. They will commandeer the blame from events, circumstances, and even other people. This commandeering of blame is a way to establish control over uncontrollable circumstances.

Abused or abandoned children will sometimes blame themselves for the abuse or the abandonment. They do this in a misguided attempt to gain some sense of control over their situation. The distorted logic is, "If I am to blame for the bad things that happen to me, then I have the power to change those bad things." Of course, this is a false belief. The child who has been abandoned or abused is not in control and is certainly not to blame. Somehow, it feels better to the child to believe they have at least a shred of control. In a similar way, dependent people may attempt to take responsibility for the bad things that happen as a way to control those bad things. Taking responsibility seems natural, since they believe themselves to blame for so much else that is wrong in their lives.

They feel responsible for fulfilling the expectations of others.

No matter how hard we try, we are not able to fulfill all the expectations of others. Sometimes we're unable because of outside circumstances. Sometimes we're unable because we don't have the capacity. Other times the expectations are just too big or too difficult to fulfill. Dependent people often take the blame when they are unable to meet the expectations of others, no matter how big the expectations. In dependency, the dependent person adopts the expectations of the other person as their own. So when the dependent person fails, they fail to meet not only the expectations of the other person but also their own. Each failure strengthens the dependent person's damaging judgment of self.

If you have a dependent personality, you may believe you must be perfect in order to be worthy of love. Perfection, to you, means perfectly meeting everyone else's needs, which is impossible. As a dependent person, you may not see the impossibility in your belief and may blame yourself when you fail to meet those expectations time and time again.

With each failure, you become more sure of being flawed and unworthy.

They are aware of the feelings of others but unsure of their own feelings.

One of the ways dependent people maintain relationships is by becoming good at reading the emotional states of others. A dependent person can become an emotional chameleon, reflecting back the other person's emotional patterns. Is the other person sad? Appear sympathetic. Is the other person happy? Appear joyful. Is the other person angry? Appear supportive. Is the other person confused? Be a sounding board. All of these responses seem right. After all, aren't we to join in with the emotional states of others?

Dependent people can appear to do this but may be unable. Dependent people can have difficulty being in touch with their own feelings because those feelings are often so negative. Afraid of their own feelings, dependent people can lock them away in deep places, choosing instead to live off the emotional states of others.

They consider the opinions and feelings of others of greater value than their own.

People with dependent personality traits often do not trust themselves, considering their opinions and feelings to be untrustworthy. They second-guess every opinion they have and constantly defer to the dominant people around them. In some ways, they are relieved when others take charge because this liberates them from the anxiety inherent in making a decision. When someone else takes over, the stress of making the wrong decision, which always looms as a high probability, is relieved. For a person with dependency traits, having an opinion can be seen as unsafe. Safety, then, is found by mirroring the thoughts, opinions, and feelings of others. Conflict is to be avoided at all cost, including the cost of speaking your own mind and laying claim to your own thoughts and opinions. Why should you fight when, deep down, you know you're going to lose? Why fight when you think you should lose?

They have a high need for validation and approval from others.

Dependent people can crave validation and approval just as desperately as an alcoholic craves a drink, a drug addict craves a hit, or a gambler craves a jackpot. When validation and approval happen, the planets align and all is right with the dependent person's universe, at least until insecurity kicks in again. For the dependent person, failure is a given; failure is the norm. So any "win," though desperately craved, is suspect as a mistake, at worst, or momentary, at best. When the thrilling rush of validation or approval is quickly quashed by insecurity, the stage is set for needing more validation and approval.

They adapt their behavior and physical appearance to the desires of others.

One of the first benchmarks of independence for a growing child is choosing what to wear. As a child, clothes are, by necessity, obtained by adults. Yet there comes that moment when a child decides between the Spiderman shirt and the dump truck shirt, between the pink top and the purple top. For many children, making that decision is exhilarating and a natural component of growing up. The more a child grows, the more that child should be given power to make decisions about what to wear or how to wear their hair. A growing, maturing child gains authority over their personal appearance.

This growing authority can become a source of angst and conflict, especially during the teenage years. However, this back and forth over personal appearance is a natural and normal part of growing up. The child learns there are rules about what is and what is not appropriate. The authority figure, generally a parent, learns to negotiate those rules and, in some cases, get rid of them altogether as a way for the child to gain needed experience in responsibility and independence.

Dependent people, though, are not always looking for responsibility and independence. To a dependent person, responsibility and independence may not equal autonomy and freedom; instead, responsibility and independence equal exposure and risk. Dependent people will often enter into relationships with opinionated, controlling people who are all too willing to dictate even the most basic functions, such as how to act and what to wear. Dependent on the relationship to provide clarity, direction, and safety, the dependent person relinquishes personal choices for the choices of the other person.

These choices of the other person need not be overtly expressed; the dependent person, who is adept at reading the emotional states of others, may use what is known about the other person as a filter for decisions. So when the dependent person hears, "That outfit looks great on you" or "I like your haircut," these positive affirmations are because the dependent person made choices they knew the other person would approve of.

They are unable to create or defend personal boundaries.

Every person has the right to determine their personal boundaries; boundaries are fundamental to a healthy sense of self. A dependent person has difficulty with personal boundaries. The only real boundary a dependent person has is to be within the boundary of a desired relationship. Apart from that, all other personal boundaries are fluid and negotiable, ready to be modified or jettisoned in order to maintain the desired relationship. A willingness to negotiate personal boundaries for a relationship creates vulnerability. Within a healthy relationship, the risk of vulnerability is low because not all personal boundaries are up for negotiation. With a dependent person, who is willing to negotiate all personal boundaries, the risk is much greater. Some personality types look to exploit this type of vulnerability. These personality types are all too willing to find out how much a dependent person is willing to give. And that pool of needs is never filled; the dependent person cannot seem to give enough to fill the other person's needs.

This type of vulnerability is often seen within sexual relationships, but that is by no means the only scenario for the exploitation of vulnerable, dependent people. There are children who will exploit the vulnerability of parents and parents who will exploit the vulnerability of children. There are family members who will exploit the vulnerability of family members and friends who will exploit the vulnerability of friends. There are employers who will exploit the vulnerability of employees and employees who will exploit the vulnerability of employers. The common denominator is that someone is willing to take everything the dependent person has to give and more, allowing the dependent person to sacrifice everything for the sake of the relationship.

They are unsure of appropriate boundaries for intimacy.

A sexual boundary is one of the most fundamental of all personal boundaries. Intimacy springs from the core of who you are as a person. Boundaries around intimacy are a primary defense to protect your sense of self. Who you allow within those intimate boundaries, as well as when, why, and how those boundaries are moved aside, is part of maintaining and growing healthy relationships.

A dependent person is ambivalent about intimate boundaries. When maintaining a relationship is paramount, maintaining intimate boundaries becomes secondary. Healthy boundaries for intimacy are determined by personal values, convictions, and religious beliefs. Dependent people who do not love or trust themselves have difficulty trusting their personal values, convictions, and religious beliefs. Dependent people are willing to listen to the reasons, rationales, and arguments of others who would seek to undermine their intimate boundaries. For a dependent person, the core benefit of intimacy is not self-expression and discovery; the core benefit of intimacy is a way to meet the desires of others. Intimacy, then, can become a tool for maintaining a relationship.

They attempt to manipulate others and situations in order to maintain relationships.

Some dependent people have a way of creating crises in which they appear to have the answers. For example, a dependent person, desperate for validation and approval from the rest of the family, may create a crisis within the family in which they are seen as the "savior" or the "fixer" of the problem. Only if a careful analysis is made of the nucleus of the crisis does the rest of the family realize the dependent person was both the fixer and the cause of the crisis.

Dependent people often feel most comfortable in the midst of crises. After all, because they do not love or trust themselves, they live in a constant state of crisis. Crisis is normal. Dependent people become used to crises and can learn to use crises to their advantage. A crisis can be an opportunity to control and manipulate others by providing whatever is needed to solve the crisis. By going above and beyond what is necessary in order to solve the crisis, dependent people create their own value, a value ironically they inwardly reject. When they are seen as the savior in a crisis, dependent people receive the validation and approval they need because these are the very things they withhold from themselves.

The greater the crisis, the greater is the possibility for validation and approval. The greater the validation and approval, the greater becomes the dependent person's value to others. The greater their value to others, the greater is their sense of being needed in the relationship. The greater their sense of being needed in the relationship, the greater their sense of safety and the less their sense of anxiety.

In truth, many dependent people do not view a crisis the same way others do. The real crisis to a dependent person is their ongoing sense of vulnerability and anxiety in the relationship. If a crisis reduces those feelings of vulnerability and anxiety, then a crisis becomes a benefit.

They have difficulty accepting challenging or disturbing truths about themselves or others.

The compulsion to hang on to the false reality created by dependent personality traits in a relationship can be strong. So often the relationships affected are core relationships with family and friends, people you dearly love. Being asked to face dependency traits in those relationships may feel like being asked to step in front of a train. Your sense of danger is real.

Dependency—and the fear that fuels it—will fight against accepting such challenging or disturbing truths about yourself and your relationships. Seeing yourself and your behaviors, actions, thoughts, and motivations as damaging to self and others is one of the most challenging truths to accept. But what is the alternative? Isn't the alternative to continue within the stranglehold of dependency in your relationships? Isn't the alternative experiencing more and more of the same?

Accepting the truth, though difficult, is your pathway to freedom. As a dependent person, isn't it true that you've spent time and energy trying to hold on to relationships that constantly threaten to slip away? To heal, you must see the value in expending time and energy in establishing relationships based on truth.

■ ■ ■

Our training and experience tell us that dependent personality traits are usually developed during childhood and into adolescence. Often these traits are used during formative years as a survival strategy when growing up with difficult, abusive, or emotionally distant or neglectful family members. Dependent people are old hands at shaky relationships because of what they experienced during childhood, so these types of relationships seem normal as adults. These types of relationships can seem so normal that a dependent person finds it difficult to identify what is wrong with a relationship. The shaky relationship itself is seen as normal, and if anything is wrong, the dependent person will automatically assume the blame.

If you had a difficult or dysfunctional childhood, you may have found it difficult or disturbing to recognize the signs of a dependent personality. Perhaps this is the first time as an adult you've thought to question the way you see yourself and others. Even though this look is difficult, we hope you've evaluated these behaviors. We hope you've been able to look at them within your relationships, including your relationship with yourself. The more of these signs you recognize, the greater your personal pattern for dependency. Placing yourself, your attitudes, and your behaviors against this template of a dependent personality is a way for you to gain insight into yourself.

We ask you to resist the temptation to use these traits as a way to assess blame. Rather, we view this as an exercise in empowerment—for it is impossible to begin to create positive changes if you see no need for change in the first place. This exercise was meant to create room for positive change in your life. We applaud your courage to walk down this challenging road.

▧ Connection Point

You've had a great deal to think about in this chapter. We've asked you to look over the traits of a dependent personality and honestly search out aspects of those traits within yourself and your relationships. In some ways, we've asked you to self-identify, which is an especially difficult task for those who seek to hide from self. We understand this is difficult, but self-identifying is a valuable and necessary step toward healing and recovery.

Self-identifying is a proven method for those dependent on things other than relationships. Think of the way an Alcoholics Anonymous meeting starts: "Hello, my name is _____, and I am an alcoholic." AA works so well because there is no hiding, no trying to avoid the truth, because the truth carries consequences, whether you choose to acknowledge the truth or not. People in AA have learned to self-identify and accept the truth of their alcoholism. This acceptance is not done to admit defeat or give in to failure but to admit the truth and reach beyond the now toward success. Those in Narcotics Anonymous or Gamblers Anonymous or Overeaters Anonymous do the same type of self-identification. They learn to accept the truth of who they are so they can gain the tools to choose a different path.

We would like you to make a proclamation similar to that of AA or NA or GA or OA. We'd like you to begin the process of acceptance and self-identification. Below, you will find the traits we've talked about. If you can identify with a trait, even a little, circle it. For any trait that you are sure you do not possess, make an X through the bullet point on the left. Start this exercise by saying the following:

My name is _____, and I am dependent in the following ways. I admit that I:

- have difficulty making everyday decisions without an excessive amount of advice and reassurance from others

- need others to assume responsibility for many major areas of my life
- find it difficult or uncomfortable to express disagreement with others because I am afraid I will lose their support or approval
- struggle to start projects or do things on my own because I do not trust my judgment or abilities
- can go to excessive lengths to obtain nurture and support from others, to the point of volunteering to do things I'd rather not do
- feel anxious or distressed when I am alone, or even thinking about being alone, because I am afraid I won't be able to handle what might happen
- urgently seek another relationship as a source of care and support when a close relationship ends
- feel better focusing attention on solving the problems of others than on my own issues
- often put the needs of others above my own needs, even if I'm really hurting or resentful
- take on the responsibility of meeting the needs of others, even if unasked or if those needs are hurtful, difficult, or even impossible
- consider myself responsible when bad things happen, even outside events and circumstances
- feel responsible for fulfilling the expectations of others and a failure if that doesn't happen
- am very aware of the needs and feelings of others but often unsure of my own needs and feelings
- consider the opinions and feelings of others as greater in value than my own

- have a high need for validation and approval from others
- will adapt my behavior and even my physical appearance to the desires of others
- find myself unable to create or defend personal boundaries because I am afraid of rejection
- am unfamiliar with or unsure of appropriate boundaries for intimacy
- attempt to manipulate others and situations in order to maintain relationships
- have difficulty accepting challenging or disturbing truths about myself or others out of a need to maintain the status quo

For every dependent trait you circled, list at least one example from your life. For any dependent trait you X'd out, list at least one example where you did the opposite. In truth, every person who honestly does this analysis will have a combination of circles and X's. Any individual, in any given situation, can display a dependent personality trait. What you are looking for are the following:

- *Pattern.* Anyone can act in a dependent way occasionally, but you are looking for an established pattern of dependency traits over time.
- *Frequency.* Ask yourself how often you resort to dependent personality traits; the greater the frequency, the greater the issue.
- *Severity.* Acting in a dependent way in some situations may have a negligible impact but in other situations could produce very damaging results. Are you able to withhold acting in a dependent manner in severe situations?

- *Disruption.* As you look over your dependency patterns, ask yourself what level of disruption these dependency patterns create in your life.

- *Denial.* As we said before, every person will have some level of dependency during their life. If after reading this chapter you circled few traits or found little to identify with, please consider the possibility that you are exhibiting the last trait of dependency, the trait of denial. There was probably a reason you were drawn to this book, and it probably wasn't so you could read it and then say to yourself, "That isn't me."

- *Hopelessness.* If after reading about the dependency traits you are experiencing a sense of heaviness or hopelessness, acknowledge those feelings. Dependent people tend to gravitate toward the worst-case scenario; they are glass-empty people. But feeling hopeless doesn't mean you are hopeless. Acknowledging your feelings doesn't mean you must give in to them. An alcoholic or a drug addict can admit to cravings without giving in to them. Acknowledging feelings of hopelessness is the first step in turning and walking away from them toward something better—hope.

Realizing you have dependent personality traits is not the end of the world; it is the beginning of healing. You cannot begin to solve a problem if you deny the problem exists. And problems, because of their very nature, do not tend to resolve on their own. Often problems are progressive; they get worse. Worse means relationships that cause heartache, anxiety, stress, frustration, disillusionment, and disappointment. Often these relationships collapse under that toxic pressure. Spouses and lovers leave. Children run away. Parents distance. Siblings vanish. Friends evaporate. Jobs disappear. Once again, the dependent person feels alone, abandoned, misunderstood, and unsafe.

When the answer to this pattern is not rooted in self but in another relationship, the search begins anew for an outside answer. Yes, recognizing your dependent personality traits is hard, but it's not any harder than the constant need to shore up, restore, or rebuild existing relationships, nor is it any harder than running in that desperate rodent's wheel of one unsatisfying relationship after another. Identifying your dependent personality traits is the beginning of a solution to the pattern of relationship dependency. You are one step closer to healing and recovery.

3

What Are the Patterns
of Relationship Dependency?

Dependent people are lonely and crave relationships because they do not like the person they are alone with—themselves. It was vital for you to understand that the key person in any relationship is you. It is also vital for you to begin to see the patterns of relationship dependency not only within each relationship but also as you move from one unhealthy relationship to another over and over again. Relationship dependency has an addictive cycle pattern.

An addictive cycle has certain established aspects, and relationship addiction is no different. For example, Melanie is an addict. She is addicted to relationships. In her mind, being in a romantic relationship is proof that she is loved. If Melanie is in a relationship, all she thinks about is how to remain in that relationship. If she is out of a relationship, all she thinks about is finding a new relationship. Through all of this, she remains perplexed at her inability to stay in a relationship.

Melanie understands she is not the most attractive person but feels she has so much to give and doesn't understand when a relationship ends and she is left alone and hurting. She wonders why she keeps choosing the wrong people to be in relationships with. Melanie laments over all the time she's wasted on people who couldn't or wouldn't love her, even when she devoted herself to them.

Though Melanie doesn't want to admit it, she's angry. She's furious at herself for making so many mistakes and bad choices. She's furious at other people for withholding their love and causing her such pain. People around her seem to be able to find love, so why not her? Melanie is convinced the right person is out there. She's tired and frustrated at the thought of another relationship ending. She's also terrified of being alone, so she just keeps looking.

When someone is addicted to relationships, they are desperate to discover another heart looking for love. This desperation leads to impulsive choices that often turn out poorly, prompting a repetitive cycle of relationship after relationship. Year after year, a dependent person burns up time, energy, and emotional and financial resources, not in get-rich-quick schemes but in get-*love*-quick schemes. Like gamblers, they are sure the next roll of the dice will produce that big win, with love and happily ever after as the payoff. When this fantasy does not happen, disillusionment sets in. Depressed and desperate to try their luck again, they gamble on yet another relationship.

■ The Addictive Cycle

Does that sound like the disappointments you've had, especially with romantic relationships? Melanie's cycle will not be the same for all those with relationship dependency. However, this cycle of relationship after relationship is a pattern for many of the people we've worked with over the years. Within this addictive cycle, we have identified eight distinct phases:

1. the search phase
2. the attraction phase
3. the relief phase
4. the anxiety phase
5. the denial phase
6. the escalation phase
7. the switching phase
8. the withdrawal phase

The Search Phase

As we've said before, people can become addicted to relationships when they believe they are unsafe alone. When a dependent person is not in a relationship, they will conduct an all-consuming search for a new relationship, just as a drug addict will search for the next hit or a gambler will wager for the next win.

While the search may be for a different *person*, it is important to note that the search is not for a different *relationship*. Those dependent on relationships tend to substitute one unhealthy or unfulfilling relationship for another, which does not result in better outcomes, thus causing the cycle to repeat. The person may look for a repeat of a previous relationship, convinced the problem was with the person instead of with the pattern.

When a dependent person goes from relationship to relationship, unknowingly, they may choose a personality type that corresponds with their dependency traits. Unfortunately, some dependent people do not feel worthy of a healthy partner or a healthy relationship because they see themselves as flawed and unlovable. A person who believes their only value is in meeting the needs of others may enter into repetitive relationships with people who have unrealistic and unreasonable demands, such as alcoholics, addicts, or those with narcissistic personality types who have a high need for control. A bond is forged between an unhealthy person who wants it all and a dependent person willing to give it all.

Why would a person knowingly enter into a relationship with an alcoholic or a drug addict, a workaholic or a controlling person, a demanding person or an abusive person? Believing that is all they deserve, some dependent people are willing to settle for second best or even lower. They do not shy away from damaged relationships because they consider themselves to be damaged. The dysfunction that comes with such damaged relationships feels comfortable, known, and expected. Subconsciously, some dependent people may be drawn to unhealthy people as a way to bind that partner to them. Dependency is strongest when it is codependency, when both partners knowingly or unknowingly contribute to the dysfunction.

The Attraction Phase

For a dependent person outside of a relationship, the stress is overwhelming. However, once a potential relationship has been found, the dependent person may engage in a compelling and overwhelming fantasy, creating an image of what the relationship will be like with the other person. At this point, the dependent person may not *see* the other person with their eyes as much as *project* an image of who they want the other person to be within their heart. The dependent person becomes convinced this relationship is the answer to all of their problems, shortcomings, and, ultimately, pain.

In the attraction phase, the dependent person pours into their vision of the relationship all of their hopes and dreams for success. They believe, this time, they've found the right person and happiness is just a heartbeat away. When speaking to others, the dependent person will extol the virtues and strength of this new relationship. If others object, they will defuse those objections and may even become defensive. Nothing, including the opinions of others, must come between them and the new relationship.

In truth, other people are not the answer to all of life's needs. There are some needs people must fulfill themselves, regardless of what others might do. These are vital needs, such as love, acceptance, approval, and forgiveness. A dependent person, however, has difficulty understanding the importance of providing these needs to self. Instead, the other person in the relationship is viewed as the provider of these needs, along with affirmation, assistance, connection, and identity—or whatever else the dependent person feels is lacking in life.

The Relief Phase

The start of a new relationship should bring a variety of experiences to both parties, but for a dependent person, the primary initial experience is one of relief. This is relief from the panic and anxiety felt when they are not in a relationship. Finding a new relationship is like coming up for air.

In some ways, the relief phase is like the honeymoon phase of a marriage. The dictionary defines the honeymoon phase as, "A pleasant period of time at the start of something (such as a relationship or a politician's term in office) when people are happy, are working with each other, etc."[1] The honeymoon phase is a known and understood human phenomenon.

A honeymoon phase, whether in marriage or in politics, isn't traditionally a long period of time. In a similar way, the relief phase is brief. The attraction phase before and the anxiety phase after create a tension that destabilizes the relief phase and causes it to be brief in duration.

In the attraction phase, the dependent person creates a mental template for what the relationship is supposed to look like, a vision of perfection and thus safety. Of course, this mental template is the sole property of the dependent person; the other person is often not actively involved in its creation and not informed of its existence, that is, unless the other person is specifically looking for a dependent person, understands that person's hidden needs, and is willing to contribute to the fantasy in order to maintain the relationship for their own reasons. Conversely, the other party may have come into the relationship with their own mental template, and perhaps the two templates are at odds with each other. Whether the two parties are working at cross-purposes or joining together out of a confluence of unhealthy needs, the relief phase is unstable and destined to self-destruct.

The Anxiety Phase

The relief phase can be marked by euphoria. Inevitably, all highs begin to break down. This breakdown occurs when the other person does not act in accordance with the preestablished mental template. The foundations of the relationship begin to shake, producing fear and anxiety. A nondependent person realizes that relationships ebb and flow, with good times and bad times. They understand there will be times when the two people are getting along and other times when they are not. A nondependent person is able to handle these times because the foundations of their relationships are based on mutual love, respect, acceptance, and forgiveness. Because the dependent person may not have these attributes in their own life, there is no pool to draw from when the relationship goes into a period of drought.

The dependent person has learned to be extraordinarily sensitive to any hint of problems in a relationship in order to adjust and diffuse those problems. With sensitivity set at such a high level, miscues and misunderstandings are bound to occur, producing more panic and anxiety. The relationship becomes treacherous, with words and actions that must be carefully navigated in order to avoid mistakes leading to pain.

When the relief phase comes crashing down, anxiety and fear, which have been waiting in the wings, rush in. The anxiety phase is a time of extreme doubt—doubting self, doubting the other person, doubting the relationship. Panic begins to set in at the thought of another relationship becoming tarnished and losing its previous glow of perfection. The thought of returning to a world of insecurity is terrifying to the dependent person, so the thought must be rejected. This rejection leads to denial.

The Denial Phase

There comes a point in a relationship when the honeymoon is over and best behavior is replaced by just-the-way-I-am attitudes. As the fog of fantasy evaporates in the heat of everyday living, glimpses can emerge of a harsher relational landscape. Glimpsing this truth can be terrifying to the dependent person, who in response will cling even more vehemently to the fantasy of the relationship.

People go through all kinds of strategies to avoid pain, both physical and psychological/emotional. Physical pain often responds favorably to medication, heat, and pressure. Psychological pain can be diffused through distraction or denial. In the denial phase, the dependent person may try both. They may attempt distraction through an addictive substance or activity in order to numb the pain. They may deny the reality of troubling issues in the relationship.

Because the thought of the relationship ending is so painful, the thought is intentionally denied. Underlying this veneer of denial, however, is a subsurface roiling with fear and anxiety. The fear and anxiety must be contained and not allowed to bubble up to the surface. When asked about the relationship, the answer is, "Everything is fine" and "What made you ask?" The denial phase is an extremely taxing phase, as the dependent person expends considerable energy to maintain the façade that everything is fine. But façades and veneers only run along the surface and do not have the depth necessary to withstand the pressure of a deteriorating relationship. Cracks appear, accelerating the destabilization of the relationship. The dependent person then must step up efforts in damage-control mode.

The Escalation Phase

For the dependent person, the relationship is everything, so nothing must be spared to maintain it. The dependent person will give up whatever is necessary—other relationships, money, time, personal preferences, and goals. The dependent person will do whatever is necessary to anticipate what might be needed to save the relationship. This is the phase when the dependent person may feel incredible pressure to shore up the shaky relationship by hemming in and attempting to contain the other person.

When the tremors of the shaky relationship become impossible to ignore, this is a time of desperation. The dependent person, caught in the instability of this phase, may begin to escalate their behavior in an attempt to bring the deteriorating relationship back to the everything-is-fine relief phase. As the tension mounts, they may even engage in sabotaging behavior, precipitating a crisis in the relationship to release tension and allow for the possibility of realignment. The dependent person may even try becoming less accommodating and more demanding as a way to force the relationship back under their control. During the escalation phase, the dependent person may circle back to any behavior or strategy that worked in the past. The effort and energy are fueled at this point not by love for the other person but by desperation and fear.

People have a tendency to recoil from intensely negative emotions and often resist being hemmed in or contained by another person. People can be like swimmers who react in surprise and anger if another swimmer attempts to use them to stay afloat. Usually those efforts are perceived as invasive, even dangerous, and are rejected. The more extreme the behavior during the escalation phase, the more likely the relationship will end badly.

The Switching Phase

The dependent person is willing to give just about anything for the relationship, except the relationship itself. Once the relationship is clearly in danger of ending, the dependent person may step out of the submissive, what-do-you-want mode and propel into an aggressive, you-owe-me mode in a last-ditch attempt to maintain the relationship. If effort and sacrifice are not enough to maintain the relationship, the dependent person may try guilt and obligation. After all, guilt and obligation are well understood by the dependent person as motivating factors.

It is during this switching phase that the dependent person may, in desperation, take off their mask and reveal the layers of need, despair, fear, and pain that lie at the core of their dependent personality. With the relationship failing, all bets are off and anything goes. During this switching phase, there is a high probability that anger will come out.

This anger is not just because of the demise of the present relationship. Pent-up anger—and all of the frustration, disappointment, and pain from past relationships—is often released as well. The dependent person may feel they are owed by the other person, owed because of all that's been given to the current relationship and owed because of all that's been given in past relationships. Someone, somewhere, sometime is supposed to pay the bill for all of that pain. In the dependent person's perfect world, this was the person who was supposed to pay and is now ducking out on the bill. The anger can be significant, fueling extreme, even violent, behavior and desperate thoughts. The escalation phase is when people destroy property, make threats to the other person or to self, or engage in stalking behaviors. When asked for an explanation for this extreme behavior, the dependent person may blame the other person for driving them to such extremes.

The Withdrawal Phase

Because their sense of self is tied to the relationship, when it ends, the dependent person is lost, alone, and vulnerable. When the relationship ends, there is no consuming distraction to deflect the intense pain and sense of devastation at the loss. The dependent person may enter into a period of withdrawal and depression. During this time, they may attempt to reestablish the relationship. If this is not successful, the pain will propel the person into another search phase, to begin the cycle again.

For people caught in the cycle of relationship dependency, the end of a relationship always seems to come as a surprise. The strength of their fantasy and the intensity of their need can obscure the truth of a relationship for months, if not years. When the truth of the instability of the relationship finally catches up with them, they are ill-prepared to face and accept the truth because they've spent so much energy avoiding it.

Withdrawal, in any addictive cycle, has an emotional component that triggers a neurochemical response. Because of this, it is possible for a dependent person to become addicted to their own release of chemicals. These chemicals are called neurotransmitters: dopamine elicits excitement; serotonin produces calm and comfort; and norepinephrine triggers the fight-or-flight response so common with crisis. (We will examine the physical effects of this cycle and how it contributes to the pattern of relationship addiction in chapter 7.)

Alone, hurting, and angry, the dependent person begins the search again. With each new search phase, they drag less positive and more negative into the next relationship. The dependent person may become emotionally and even physically weaker and is, therefore, more susceptible to abusive, manipulative, and controlling personality types and people ready to pounce on someone so vulnerable. With this addictive, merry-go-round cycle of relationships, there is no music, no laughter, no happy ending.

Wheel within a Wheel

Before we end this discussion of the addictive cycle that can occur with relationship dependency, it is important to note that not all cycles are complete. Some dependent people will find themselves stuck, going round and round, experiencing the cyclic highs and lows but within the same relationship. For these people, the escalation and withdrawal phases are "successful," in that the relationship does not end but cycles back to the attraction or relief phase as the other person relents to remain in the relationship.

Consider, as an extreme example, the cycle of an abusive relationship in which one partner physically hits the other person. Once the abuse happens, the offending partner swears they are sorry and "it will never happen again." The abusive partner makes all kinds of amends and again courts the other person with their best behavior, replicating the conditions of the attraction phase and allowing the fantasy to be reestablished temporarily. This wheel within a wheel may go on for years, even decades. But the odd status quo achieved within this cycle can be thrown out of balance. A precipitating event, such as an illness, the loss of another relationship, the death of a parent, an adult child moving out, or the loss of a job, can cause the house of cards to crumble.

A cycle of addiction due to relationship dependency can occur from one relationship to another, and it can occur within a single relationship. When addiction is present within an ongoing relationship, often the relationship—and the addiction that forges it—is fortified by both parties, acting within their own respective needs. The joint addictive/dependent patterns tend to bind even a shaky relationship together, at least for a period of time. The longer the period of time, the greater the pressure and the more likely a precipitating event will cause a fatal blow to the relationship, even after the two people have been together for many years.

■ **Connection Point**

For an alcoholic to recover, they must begin to view alcohol as a poison and not as a promise. For a pathological gambler to recover, they must begin to view a wager as a loss no matter the outcome. To end a relationship cycle, a dependent person must begin to view the pattern of revolving relationships not as a doorway but as a dead end. If you recognize that you are caught in this cycle, or caught in the wheel-within-a-wheel spin of an ongoing relationship, you must see the cycle for what it is. Movement is not necessarily progress, and it is possible to expend a great deal of energy moving backward.

We would like you to take a good, hard look at your relationships—your current relationships as well as your past relationships. Do not limit yourself to romantic relationships. A romantic relationship may not be where you are most likely to seek validation, approval, or acceptance. You may look to work relationships, friendships, or relationships with family members for these things.

Write down your significant relationships and then answer the following questions:

1. Why are these relationships important to you?
2. Are the relationships you have right now enough? Why or why not?
3. What would your ideal relationship look like?
4. Have you ever experienced an ideal relationship? If so, with whom?
5. Do you seem to seek out the same sort of people to enter into a relationship with?
6. Do you put pressure on yourself to "fix" your relationship failures by finding the "right" person?
7. After you suspect a relationship may not be turning out as you planned, what do you do to keep it going?
8. Is there anything you would not do to maintain a desired relationship? If so, what?
9. Have you been surprised when a relationship ended, feeling you had no warning?
10. When one relationship ends, are you afraid you won't be able to find another one?

Fueling the addictive cycle of relationship dependency is fear. Fear is what compels the addiction and keeps you strapped to that merry-go-round or spinning wheel. To stop the spinning and get off, you must discover your fears, find the path that allows you to overcome them, and move forward.

4

What Are the Fears
of Relationship Dependency?

The cycle of relationship dependency is vicious, whether a person is repeating the same pattern over and over again within an existing relationship or cycling from one person to another, continually attempting to re-create the "perfect" relationship. Relationship dependency is like living life on a tightrope. Yes, a relationship provides a surface to stand on, but that surface is incredibly thin and inherently unstable. Dependent people use other people like a tightrope walker uses a long pole, as a way to keep balanced. The concentration necessary to live life on a relational tightrope is consuming and exhausting. One small slip can spell disaster, and the possibility always exists of the pole tilting, threatening to send the dependent person into a relationship abyss.

What kind of a life is this? Why would anyone choose to climb back on that wire again and again? With tightrope walkers, the goal of traversing the tightrope is to success-fully navigate from one platform to another platform. That's why we watch; we want to see the walker move from safety to safety and are relieved when it happens. In the circus, the platforms represent safety and the wire represents danger. Relationship addiction may seem like a circus, but it is not. Unlike in a circus, in relationship dependency, it is the wire—the relationship—that represents safety and standing alone on the platform that represents danger. In relationship dependency, safety and danger are confused.

If you are a dependent person, fear may propel you out onto the tightrope of unstable relationships. Fear is one of the most compelling motivators for human action and be-havior. But fear does not always produce actions or behaviors that contribute to safety. Fear can be reactive not responsive, especially primal, gut-level fear. A person may be so terrified that they freeze when they should move. A person may be so terrified that they move when they should stay still. Fear propels action, but that action can be the opposite of what is truly needed for safety.

The Fears of Relationship Dependency

At the heart of relationship dependency is fear gone wrong, with fear producing the opposite of what is truly needed for a person to have safe and secure relationships. Through our work, we've identified nine basic fears that weave through the pattern of relationship dependency. Each fear is a platform, and a dependent person ventures out onto the razor-thin wire of relationship dependency as a way to move from perceived danger to perceived safety. These fears are:

1. fear of exposure
2. fear of emptiness
3. fear of abandonment
4. fear of rejection
5. fear of insignificance
6. fear of losing security
7. fear of losing connection
8. fear of loss of control
9. fear that self is not enough

Fear of Exposure

Susan hated corporate functions of any kind. Being in a group of people meant the risk that she would spill something on herself or say something wrong. Susan supposed she could pretend to be ill, but it was too late for that. She was trapped. She just needed to stay close to Paul, watch him, and take his lead. They weren't really interested in her anyway. Her husband was the shining star. Susan was happy to disappear into his aura. That way she could keep herself safe.

If you have dependent personality traits, the last thing you want is a spotlight. Spotlights are glaring, eye-tearing, heated places of exposure. Spotlights reveal bumps and bulges and spots of imperfection. When you feel you are a damaged person, exposure means the potential for ridicule and rejection by others. If people see you the way you really are, they will see how unlovable you are.

A dependent person feels contaminated with imperfections and seeks ways to conceal them. One of the ways to conceal self is to avoid situations that might risk exposure. When that is not possible, the other way to conceal self is to slip into the covering shadow of another person. A dependent person can feel sheltered within such a relationship. In the shadow of another person, they may not be seen, but neither will they be exposed.

Fear of Emptiness

In high school, they'd called themselves the Four Musketeers. Ron's goal was just to be a part of the group. Being a part of the group served him well during high school and beyond. Ron didn't have to take any initiative because he always knew what he would be doing; all he had to do was ask Jimmy. For almost half of his life, Ron had filled up that life with Jimmy and Steve and Nathan. If the gang split up and went their separate ways, where would that leave Ron? Nowhere, that's where. Ron didn't know who he was without them.

When a dependent person has no sense of self, if others are absent, no one is home. If you are a dependent person, without the constant affirmation and companionship of other people, you don't really know who you are. Your identity becomes tied to relationships. Without relationships, you may feel empty, as if you could just disappear. Being terrified of this sense of nothingness, this loss of identity, is understandable. Without a strong sense of self, you can become lost, feeling unwanted and invisible.

Fear of Abandonment

Andrea was in turmoil. Everything between them had been going so well and now this—Ryan couldn't go out Thursday because he was supposedly visiting an out-of-town friend.

Frantic, she tried to think back over the past few weeks, which was hard when her mind was in such a panic. Was there something she had said that he'd taken wrong? Any odd looks or cross words? She should have known things were going too well. There was always something that caused things to fall apart. She could pretend nothing was wrong, but what if something was wrong? Andrea couldn't think of anything else to try.

A nondependent person would have no problem thinking of what else Andrea could try. She could try accepting Ryan's explanation, wish him a fun time with his friend, and find something else to do on Thursday. But if you have dependent personality traits, this simple approach isn't so simple. When you're dependent, you can become consumed with a constant fear of losing relationships. Any glitch, any stray from the fantasized norm of the relationship becomes a great cause for concern, fear, and consuming rumination.

One of the consequences of dependency is that you can take an ordinary occurrence, like a last-minute change in plans, as proof of disaster. An old friend coming into town, having to work late, or even the onset of a cold can be viewed with the utmost suspicion. If there is a truth to be found, you fear it lies with you being abandoned, again.

Abandonment in relationships is an overarching theme in dependency. Because people have a tendency to see what they look for, if you're looking for examples of abandonment, you will find examples of abandonment. Once you find those examples, you go into fix-it mode, recommitting to doing everything "perfectly" in order to hold on to the relationship. Or you panic and exit the relationship prematurely to avoid further pain. You may even react with anger and blame, trying to guilt the other person into apologizing.

While the first option may not register with the other person immediately, the second and third options will often appear to come out of left field. The other person may be baffled why you would leave the relationship over something trivial. And if you act in anger over something so trivial, the other person may react with similar hostility, leading to the end of the relationship. If the relationship ends this way, the only thing that is validated is your fear of abandonment.

Fear of Rejection

The end-of-the-year awards celebration was just a few weeks away. As far as Adam was concerned, he was already a winner because he wasn't a contender. If Adam ever won an award, he would then be expected to do so again, and that was just too much pressure. Better to let Rick take the credit and the stress. Adam would sit in the back and root for Rick, even if Adam had done most of the work.

If you are a dependent person, you find it hard to trust in your own value or worth. Feeling worthless, you may live in constant fear of being discovered as such and rejected. This fear of rejection is why you may enter into relationships with people who freely co-opt your ideas and work product as their own. While others would resent another person claiming credit for work they'd done, you don't seek recognition because recognition carries the unacceptable risk of rejection.

For a dependent person, rejection must be avoided at all costs. Paradoxically, a dependent person who routinely does just about anything to avoid rejection by others consistently rejects self. A dependent person, so sure of their own worthlessness, can become hyper-focused on rejection. This fear of rejection can manifest itself in romantic relationships but can also exist in work relationships. A dependent person may take a job that is beneath their ability level, preferring to overperform in secret rather than risk the danger of underperforming in public.

Fear of Insignificance

Darlene closed her eyes, but the hated vision, the vision she kept trying to avoid, intruded. She was nineteen all over again, standing, shaking in the living room, explaining to her parents that she was getting married. "He'll dump you in a heartbeat," her father had predicted. "And when he does, don't come running back here." Of course, he'd been right; her father was always right about her. That marriage hadn't lasted a year, the second one only a little longer. This next one had to last. She'd do whatever she had to in order to make it last. Her father always told her that nobody would want her. Someday, somehow, with someone, she was going to prove him wrong.

Sometimes in relationship dependency, the person in a relationship is interchangeable; being in a relationship is paramount. The fact of the relationship validates the dependent person. You may be a dependent person who feels the pressure to "set the record straight" through your next relationship. If this is you, you may have determined there will be no more failures as you set about to locate a suitable partner. Unfortunately for you, sometimes the type of person who has the most to gain from staying in a relationship is the type of person who has the most to gain from staying in an *unhealthy* relationship. You may end up settling for an unhealthy person, concluding—consciously or unconsciously—the needier the person, the greater the chance for success, with success defined as being in a relationship. Significance, then, is gained through the relationship and not through a particular person. As the saying goes, any port in a storm. The difficulty with this strategy is that the needier the other person, the stormier the relationship.

Fear of Losing Security

Ruth insisted they go to counseling together. What was Kurt to do? Say no? What Ruth wanted, Ruth got. Ruth had wanted someone to say, "Yes, dear" and "No, dear" and "How high should I jump, dear." Kurt was more than willing to do all those things. He was terrified of the responsibility of providing for a family and earning a living. He could contribute, but she was the one making the big money. Her job was the one that counted. Kurt had traded in importance for security—security from responsibility, security from expectations. And now that security was threatened by this stupid counseling. When the counselor told him how high he had to jump, he'd do it, anything to keep Ruth happy, even if making her happy meant he was miserable.

With strong feelings of abandonment and rejection, without an inner anchor of value or self-worth, you may find your security tied to a relationship. Because, as a dependent person, safety is such a strong need, you're willing to give up quite a bit of yourself in exchange. Because you don't value yourself, you figure you haven't given up much.

Do you remember when you became an adult? That is a rite of passage most young people eagerly anticipate. They envision a life in which they can make their own choices and set their own course in life. But freedom to make your own choices carries the real risk of making poor ones. Setting your own course in life can sometimes lead to going offtrack. Becoming an adult is a time of testing, a time of maturing. Becoming an adult can be messy and sometimes painful.

Becoming an adult is not universally longed for, especially if you have dependent traits. Instead of seeing the reward of adulthood, you see the risk. You may resist entering into adult relationships, preferring the shelter of existing family relationships, preferring quasi-adolescence—old enough to make some decisions but scared enough to avoid most. When you do enter into relationships, you may find yourself choosing strong-willed people who take over responsibility for you. You choose these types of relationships because they provide structure and protection from the perceived dangers of full adulthood.

Fear of Losing Connection

The doctor had not been optimistic. The remaining time was unbelievably short. Why now? Mary thought to herself. Of course, she knew her mother couldn't live forever, but she always thought they would have more time. How could ten or fifteen years turn into just a few months? Mary would do whatever she could in those last few months to make sure her mother was comfortable and cared for. Caring for Mom had always been her job. The others had left home, started families and lives elsewhere. Not Mary; Mary was still there and would be to the end. To Mary, losing her mother was the end. Losing her mother would be the end of her usefulness, the end of her purpose in the world. Who was she without that?

Without a connection to self, a dependent person relies on relationships to be their connection to the world. If you see yourself only through the eyes of others, without others you cannot see yourself. You are blinded and cannot see a life without that relationship. Losing the relationship, the connection, and living life adrift are terrifying.

Fear of Loss of Control

Somebody upstairs thought it was a good idea for Randy to show the new guy around the plant. As if Randy had the time to show some guy around. Why were the higher-ups always doing stuff like that? Bring in a new guy, and things got turned upside down. Who knew what this guy would want to change? New bosses always meant changes. If the truth be told, Randy could run the plant himself and did, when people just left him alone. Randy looked at the clock on the wall and took a deep breath. He'd be pleasant, spout the company line. This wouldn't be a complete waste of time. Randy would use it to get a read on the new guy and figure out how much trouble he was likely to cause. If anyone was going to be uncomfortable at this job, it was not going to be Randy.

Because dependent people live in such an ongoing state of fear, they will go to great lengths to establish order and a sense of control over their surroundings. Does that sound like you? Do you recognize those desires within yourself? When disaster is seen as only one misstep away, it's understandable that you would seek to control others. You may be the type of person who feels safe only when you can control those around you.

This need for control can seem counterintuitive for people who do not have a strong sense of self. But if you do not have a strong sense of self, you may substitute a strong sense of *safety*. If you do not trust yourself, then you are left to trust in others to avoid danger. Nondependent people welcome outside people or events into their worlds because they carry their safety within their sense of self. Dependent people are susceptible to suspicion of outside people or events because they fear those people or events will cause a loss of safety. If you do not feel safe within yourself, you construct a scaffold of safety around yourself, often using routine, tradition, and rules. The authority, then, comes from the rules and not from you, thus deflecting away any responsibility. If you are dependent, you may use these outside sources of authority to coerce compliance and maintain control over people and situations.

Fear That Self Is Not Enough

Just stay busy, Patricia told herself. Keep moving. Bury yourself in work. Do as much as you can and more so. Everything was falling apart in Patricia's life but her job. Her husband was threatening to leave, again. Her daughter wasn't speaking to her, again. When Patricia was at work, she could forget all of those family problems. Just keep your head down and do your job, she told herself. There had to be someplace in this world where she was worth something. It wasn't at home right now, that was for sure. Stay busy. Bury yourself in work. Do as much as you can and more so. She was just so tired.

■　■　■

Dependent people can expend a great deal of time, energy, and thought running away from themselves and their problems. A dependent person who feels empty of value and worth may turn away from value in who they are and instead look for value in what they do. This shift is a way for the dependent person to say, "Don't look at who I am because who I am will never be enough; look instead at what I can do." Value and worth are moved away from self and moved toward production and activity. When a person is constantly moving away from self, that person is always on the move.

When you run away from yourself, then you are always on the run, which is exhausting. There is a point when fear no longer is effective, and that point is the point of exhaustion. Are you exhausted? Are you tired of running and ending up nowhere good? You may find yourself at the brink of utter exhaustion, continually attempting to control people and circumstances to create safety. Within that frenzy, there can be no moment of relaxation.

This is living on the edge, and dependent people live on the edge of fear at all times. Under a constant barrage of fight-or-flight adrenaline, you can career from crisis to crisis, convinced you are one step away from total disaster, one step away from being revealed as unworthy, without value, unlovable, damaged.

You need to ask yourself, Why would I agree to such a difficult life? Why would I willingly place myself within such difficult relationships or continue to allow my relationships to be so difficult? One of your answers may be fear—fear of being exposed, fear of being empty, fear of being abandoned, fear of being rejected, fear of being considered insignificant, fear of losing security, fear of losing connection, fear of losing control, fear of not being enough. Dependent people can live beneath the monstrous shadow of fear that looms over their lives, unaware that what they really fear is their own shadow.

■ Connection Point

What are you afraid of? Do you know? Or are you afraid to uncover your fears? Many people go to great lengths to hide their fears, not only from others but also from themselves.

Facing a fear is best done from a position of safety. Dependent people rarely ever feel safe and, if so, only for a fleeting period of time. This makes facing fears an especially challenging task for those with dependency traits. Challenging, but not impossible. Challenging, but necessary.

At the end of the last chapter, we asked you to think about your significant relationships. For each relationship you listed, we'd like you to write down answers to the following questions:

1. If your true self was exposed in this relationship, what do you fear would happen?
2. What is it about yourself that you are afraid for this person to know or see?
3. If this relationship was to end, would you feel you'd lost a part of yourself? If so, which part of yourself would you lose?
4. If this relationship was to end, which parts of yourself would you keep? Name those parts.
5. Are you afraid of losing this relationship? If so, why?
6. What would it say about you if you lost this relationship?
7. Is this a relationship you feel "worthy" of having?

8. Do you live in fear that the truth about yourself will be discovered and you'll lose this relationship? If so, what is that truth?

9. Does this relationship make you feel more special than you know you are?

10. If you lost this relationship, in what ways would you lose significance?

11. Do you need this relationship to help you feel secure? In what way?

12. Within this relationship, how do you define security?

13. How true is this statement: With this relationship, I'm somebody; without this relationship, I'm nobody. Why is the statement true for this relationship?

14. What are you willing to give in order to hold on to this relationship?

15. What are you not willing to give in order to hold on to this relationship?

16. When this relationship feels out of control to you, what do you do to bring the relationship back under control?

17. When you are with only yourself, how do you feel?

18. Complete this sentence: In this relationship, I wish I were more . .

19. Complete this sentence: In this relationship, I wish I were less . . .

Depending on the number of relationships you listed and the honesty you give to each question, this could be a lengthy exercise. Still, we encourage you to find and take the time. Fears are quite adept at hiding in the back corners of your mind. When fears do reveal themselves, they will often masquerade as something else, such as anger, frustration, irritation, or impatience. At the core of each of these is a fear. When you are angry, what are you afraid of? When you are frustrated, what are you afraid of? When you are irritated, what are you afraid of? When you are impatient, what are you afraid of?

Dependent fear keeps you immobile when you should move.

Dependent fear keeps you moving when you should stop.

Dependent fear tells you not to listen when you should pay attention.

Dependent fear tells you to look away when you should face forward.

Dependent fear wants to control your life in a misguided attempt to keep you safe. But dependent fear does not always understand what is safe and what is dangerous.

Dependent fear is misguided and misunderstands because dependent fear is not based in truth.

Dependent fear is based on a lie, even many lies, often told to you or experienced by you as you were growing up. These childhood lies can grow up into full-fledged fears when you are an adult. As a child, you may have been terrified of the dark, assuming a lack of light meant an abundance of danger. The force of that fear may still press against you as an adult. Yet, as an adult, you are better equipped to press back against that fear, with understanding and maturity. As a frightened child, dark can seem an endless night. As an adult, you can learn to see past the dark and toward the dawn.

5

How Does Emotional Abuse Contribute to Relationship Dependency?

Most people have an understanding of the concept of physical abuse. They see the battered woman or the beaten child and consider those situations horrific examples of physical abuse. Most people also have an understanding of the concept of sexual abuse. They see the rape victim or children caught in sex trafficking and categorize those situations as unacceptable examples of sexual abuse.

Some lines of physical and sexual behavior are clear and definitive, yet other lines may be blurred. What about the parent who spanks a child for misbehaving? In some sectors, such behavior is acceptable, even encouraged, yet in other sectors, such behavior is considered barbaric. What about the spouse who barters sex for other items in the marriage?

In some sectors, such behavior is considered normal, yet in others, such behavior is considered manipulative and exploitive. Within that continuum, how do you define what is and is not abusive?

In the case of physical and sexual abuse, though the lines may be blurred in some situations, over the past centuries and more recent decades, society has continued to refine what is and is not acceptable behavior. Physical abuse and sexual abuse, as concepts, are part of the cultural landscape. The concept of emotional abuse, however, has not advanced as far or been on the cultural consciousness as long. For many, emotional abuse remains a murkier concept.

Defining emotional abuse is important. As a culture, we need to continue the conversation about emotional abuse, in general, and what constitutes emotional abuse, specifically. In this chapter, we will attempt to contribute to that cultural conversation by discussing emotional abuse in regard to relationship dependency. In doing so, we hope to help fill in the picture of the characteristics and effects of emotional abuse. We believe emotional abuse in our culture is pervasive and damaging and as relevant a topic of discussion as physical and sexual abuse.

Brian Greene says, "I believe the process of going from confusion to understanding is a precious, even emotional, experience that can be the foundation of self-confidence."[1] Put the opposite way, when a person goes from understanding to a state of confusion, it is an emotional experience that can be the foundation for the destruction of self-confidence. Emotional abuse, as we will present it in this chapter, is a major source of confusion, including relational confusion, leading to the destruction of self.

Emotional abuse undercuts a person's foundational self-confidence and love of self and replaces them with confusion about self-worth, value, justice, mercy, and love. Emotional abuse, then, is extremely important, which brings us back to the question at the heart of the cultural conversation: What constitutes emotional abuse? Further, when and how are emotions abused? If physical and sexual abuse have a range, on which good people may profess disagreement, is there a range to emotional abuse? What is that range? With physical abuse, there are bruises and welts, scratches and scars. With sexual abuse, there is unwanted or unacceptable intrusion and sexualization. How can we quantify the damage when attitudes do the wounding or when actions leave no physical trace?

Over the years, both of us as clinicians have come to recognize the pervasive damage to the mind, soul, and spirit of a person who experiences emotional abuse. Emotional abuse is real and, in our experience, more pervasive than either physical or sexual abuse. Emotional abuse almost always accompanies physical or sexual abuse, but emotional abuse can occur without anyone lifting a finger. Emotional abuse can be armchair abuse. Emotional abuse can be an aggressive yell or passive silence. Emotional abuse is often created through the covert absence of something good instead of the overt presence of something bad.

Because we live in a broken world in which people do not—and cannot—always govern their own actions or words, emotional abuse is far too common. When a father hauls off and slugs a defiant child, using adult strength, energy, and anger to inflict damage, we readily condemn such behavior as physical abuse. But what about the father who uses adult sarcasm from a position of influence and authority to belittle, demean, and ridicule a defiant child? No punch is thrown; no eye is blackened or lip split. Yet that child has sustained an emotional and relational injury.

Emotional injuries are sustained in relationships, even among those of us who should know better. Both of us have memories of times we emotionally injured those we love out of frustration, anger, selfishness, or fatigue. All people, unfortunately, have the capacity to be unkind. But when is the line crossed between acts of unkindness and emotional abuse? When does unkindness devolve into cruelty and the intent to harm? Before we link the damage of emotional abuse to the characteristics of relational dependency, we first need to explain our corner of this cultural conversation by offering our definition of emotional abuse.

■ Emotional Abuse Defined

Emotional abuse is a pattern of behavior that involves words, action, or inaction (i.e., neglect) specifically designed to eat away at another person's sense of self. Emotional abuse is a pattern of intentional infliction of emotional injury onto another person. Emotional abuse is the elevation of self—desires, wants, preferences, or opinions—through the demotion, belittlement, or dismissal of others.

When we talk about the elevation of self as a negative, this may seem somewhat contradictory to the concepts of self-love and self-worth we've explained so far. Emotional abuse is the elevation of self at the complete and total expense of others. Emotional abuse places self on a precarious pedestal and then vehemently guards that tottering position through a snarling, vicious defense that seeks to throw others off into a relational abyss. Healthy self-love is diametrically different. Healthy self-love creates a stable, broad plateau of peace, acceptance, and understanding around self and then invites others to join and share in that sacred space.

Emotional abuse is not a by-product of self-love. Emotional abuse is not love of any kind but rather the polar opposite of love. At times, emotional abuse will attempt to cloak itself as love, justifying its selfish motives as challenging to others but ultimately loving. People, especially young children, can become confused by this subterfuge and mistake love for the actions, attitudes, and behaviors that are actually emotionally abusive. Children who are told these emotionally abusive actions, attitudes, and behaviors are "loving" become confused about what real love looks, acts, and feels like. For example, when a child is consistently yelled at by a parent, that child is experiencing emotional abuse. But when the parent explains that the reason for their frustration and irritation is a desire for the child to do better, the child may come to believe this is how you encourage motivation in others. When the actions, attitudes, and behaviors of emotional abuse are mistaken by a child as loving, that child is susceptible to carrying those mistaken beliefs into adulthood.

We have said that emotional abuse can be difficult to define. We have also said that emotional abuse is the polar opposite of love. While society is still working out a comprehensive definition of emotional abuse, as Christian therapists, we believe we have a divinely inspired definition of love. Understanding love helps us to understand love's polar opposite—emotional abuse. The apostle Paul defines love in the following terms:

Love is patient, love is kind. It does not envy, it does not boast, it is not proud. It does not dishonor others, it is not self-seeking, it is not easily angered, it keeps no record of wrongs. Love does not delight in evil but rejoices with the truth. It always protects, always trusts, always hopes, always perseveres. (1 Cor. 13:4–7)

If emotional abuse is the antithesis of love, then we can use this definition to help define the parameters of emotional abuse.

- Emotional abuse is perpetually impatient, never satisfied or accepting.
- Emotional abuse uses envy to create negative feelings and actions toward others.
- Through boasting and bragging, emotional abuse elevates self by demeaning others.
- Emotional abuse heralds its own actual or perceived successes while failing to recognize the value of others.
- Emotional abuse honors itself by dishonoring others.
- Emotional abuse does not compromise or work with others for mutual benefit.
- Anger fuels the words, actions, and attitudes of emotional abuse.
- Emotional abuse is a perverted historian, making sure to rub others' wrongs continually in their faces while refusing to accept or acknowledge its own failings.
- Emotional abuse looks forward to any opportunity to strike at another person and strenuously avoids allowing other opinions, perspectives, or viewpoints to interject a different interpretation of truth.

- The only thing emotional abuse seeks to protect is its right to wound.
- Emotional abuse is founded on deep suspicion and distrust of others.
- Emotional abuse provides no hope, preferring to pass final and absolute judgment on the wrongness of others in spite of any evidence to the contrary.

If there is one thing love and emotional abuse appear to have in common, it is the characteristic of perseverance. Emotional abuse can be generational, persevering as common practice from generation to generation. Yet in the final analysis, authentic love does have the power to conquer emotional abuse, as people do have the capacity to change and choose differently. And even if the emotional abuse perseveres, love is able to diminish and reverse its damaging effects.

The apostle John defines love this way: "God is love" (1 John 4:8). God is the epitome of love, and through that love he creates a stable, broad plateau of peace, acceptance, and understanding, inviting us through Christ to join him and share in that sacred relational space. God meant for healthy self-love to mirror his space, his characteristics, and his invitation to others to join in relationship.

Sadly, we fall short. Some of us fall short occasionally and deeply regret it. Some fall short continually and think that's normal. When falling short and engaging in the behaviors of emotional abuse are viewed as normal, emotional abuse can become a perpetuating pattern, repeating itself from one generation to the next, from one relationship to the next. The pattern is replicated so often that finding the source of the pattern can prove difficult. However, our clinical years of experience tell us that this pattern of emotional abuse that can lead to relational dependency often begins in childhood.

The Generational Power of Emotional Abuse

To help illustrate the generational power of emotional abuse, we'll use the scenario of Drew, Amy, and Caleb. They represent many aspects of the generational emotional abuse we've observed as therapists. While their story may not be your story, pay attention to how you feel as you read about Drew, Amy, and Caleb. Note whom you identify with in each situation. Can you see yourself in parts of the story? Can you see other people in parts of the story? If you could tell your own story, what would it be?

Drew felt sick all day at school. He wished he were like Paul and Kevin, who never had to worry about bringing home their report cards. They were smart; he was not. Schoolwork was hard, and Drew often stayed after school to work with Mrs. Linderman. She was so nice and helpful. She never seemed rushed and never tried to do three other things while she worked with him on his grammar or science. Homework wasn't that way at home. Drew's mother always said she'd help him, but then something would come up or she'd be working on something else as Drew sat at the kitchen table. When Drew would ask for help, his mother would exhale loudly, make a big deal of putting down whatever she was doing, and go over to see what it was this time.

At least his mom was better than his dad. Drew knew better than to ask his dad for help. His dad seemed to enjoy making him squirm, making Drew stand in front of him as he slowly opened Drew's report card. If Drew's grades rose, they could always be better, according to his dad. If his grades dropped, his dad would yell and complain how Drew was never going to amount to much with grades like these. Drew's dad would call over his mother, who seemed to disappear every time report cards came home. His dad would shake the paper in her face and loudly ask her what she was going to do about it. Drew's mom would just shrug and walk off, as if saying it wasn't her fault Drew was stupid; there was nothing she could do. Drew felt the same way. Hopeless. At night, he'd dream about what it must be like to be Paul or Kevin, or just about anybody else.

The impact of emotional abuse is particularly harmful and long lasting when the abuse is experienced in childhood, as it imprints on the person a poor self-image that infiltrates behaviors and choices for the rest of their life. Of course, this includes behaviors and choices made in the creation and management of relationships.

■ ■ ■

Amy exhaled loudly and plopped down her purse on the kitchen counter. Drew knew she was frustrated because he was having trouble pulling up the website for directions to their accountant. They saw the guy only twice a year; how was he supposed to remember where he worked? Besides, the office had moved in the past six months. With a stern warning that all of this was going to make them late, Amy demanded to know why Drew hadn't looked up the website sooner, "like a normal person." Scooting him off the computer, she took over and deftly pulled up the website and printed the directions. Grabbing them off the printer in the office, she snatched up her purse, proclaiming they were going to be late and she would drive. Drew felt about half an inch tall. He couldn't do anything right. She'd do all the driving, and when they got to the accountant, she'd do all the talking. Drew would just sit there and try not to say something stupid. Story of his life.

Children are not usually born into this world convinced of their own incompetency. Children are usually born into this world with a natural wonder, sweetness, innocence, and unbridled belief in the possibility of themselves and of tomorrow. Children, in short, are usually born into this world imbued with hope. Jesus articulated this hope when he admonished the disciples by saying, "Let the little children come to me, and do not hinder them, for the kingdom of heaven belongs to such as these" (Matt. 19:14). Hope is the divine inheritance of children, but their earthly inheritance can consist of anything but hope. Sadly, hope can be taken away from children in the very environment, within the very relationship, that was meant to bolster, sustain, and support that divine hope—within the family.

When family relationships are the breeding ground for emotional abuse, hope, belief, and possibility are robbed from children. Instead of being loved, those children are judged. Instead of being nurtured, those children are demeaned. Instead of being emotionally supported, those children are emotionally battered. Instead of being protected, those children are preyed upon. Instead of looking forward to the future, those children come to distrust tomorrow. Could you have stopped trusting in tomorrow because you were robbed of the joy of the future as a child?

Children react to this emotional abuse in a variety of ways. Some swallow it. Some rebel against it. Some believe all of it.

All believe some of it and are scarred. This scarring as a child can create an environment for relational dependency as an adult. An emotionally abused person looks to other people, to an outside relationship, to provide approval, validation, assurance, relief, and significance because these emotional assets were stolen from them in childhood. In a terrible conundrum, an emotionally abused person looks to others to validate self, but these outside relationships are compromised by the effects of the abuse.

When an emotionally abused person lacks a sense of value, worth, and significance, they are constantly fearful that the needed relationship will disappear. Because they do not see themselves as worthy of love, they have a relentless fear that the other person will leave. Therefore, they end up maintaining tight, obsessive, and manipulative control over the relationship in order to avoid what they fear is eventually inevitable. This stranglehold on the relationship, the obsessive, manipulative control by the emotionally abused person, can end up being emotionally abusive itself, with the person unwittingly perpetuating the patterns as an adult that were so damaging to them as a child.

■ ■ ■

Drew was furious. He knew Caleb could do better; he just wasn't trying. Sternly, he told his red-faced third-grader no video games until his math grade came up. Caleb tried to argue that he'd done well in English and social studies, but Drew was determined not to be sidetracked. Caleb took after Amy, which meant he was fully capable of pulling all A's if he would just apply himself. For once, Drew and Amy were in full agreement. Caleb tried again to argue, but Amy let him know, in no uncertain terms, that if he continued to be disrespectful, his punishment could get much worse. At that point, Caleb shut his mouth and marched off to his room, but not before Drew thought he saw the glimmer of tears on his stone-faced eight-year-old. Amy looked unmoved by Caleb's distress, but Drew felt a sudden wave of nausea. Where did that come from? Was he coming down with something?

Emotional abuse can look like other things—a stern warning, an offhand comment, a joke, a legitimate concern. Discerning emotional abuse can be difficult and can require looking past the initial action, attitude, or behavior to the outcomes produced by them. In the fall, when leaves are gone, all trees tend to look the same. It is only in summer, when each tree bears its fruit—bears its outcomes—that a stern-warning tree can be differentiated from an emotionally abusive tree. Jesus put the concept this way: "No good tree bears bad fruit, nor does a bad tree bear good fruit. Each tree is recognized by its own fruit. People do not pick figs from thornbushes, or grapes from briers" (Luke 6:43–44). Taken individually, actions can be rationalized, excused, or justified. But emotional abuse, as a pattern, produces certain definable outcomes. By looking at the outcomes, the fruit, we can recognize emotional abuse.

What are the signs of emotional abuse? The list below comes from a book I (Dr. Gregg) wrote almost twenty years ago called *Healing the Scars of Emotional Abuse*. Over the past twenty years, both of us (Dr. Gregg and Dr. Tim) have become even more convinced of the validity of these signs.

◼ Signs of Emotional Abuse

Signs of emotional abuse include actions, attitudes, and behaviors that:

- intentionally make another person feel worthless and/ or intentionally cause hurt
- put the blame for one's mistakes on another person
- minimize or dismiss the other person's point of view
- threaten or hint at physical or sexual abuse
- devolve into fits of rage and intense anger
- fail to fulfill commitments or promises made or implied
- use intentional lying to avoid responsibility for the truth
- refuse to acknowledge the other person's feelings
- verbally or physically humiliate the other person through inappropriate gestures, comments, or jokes
- use shame or guilt to manipulate the actions of the other person
- do not allow the other person to articulate their feelings
- deny the person access to their personal possessions or pets
- withhold appropriate financial resources
- are a variation of the silent treatment
- display extreme ranges of mood, creating uncertainty and fear
- involve making conditional agreements in which the conditions keep changing so the person does not have to fulfill the agreement
- involve a hostile or sarcastic tone of voice

- are critical of each action, attitude, or behavior of the other person
- show that the person views others as a part of their own personality as opposed to individuals with their own thoughts, feelings, and opinions
- belittle, humiliate, marginalize, and/or ignore the other person

Again, no one is perfect, and each one of us is guilty of engaging in emotionally abusive behavior at times. Each person must evaluate the content of their relationship interactions and determine if the line has been crossed from occasional unkindness to a pattern of emotionally abusive behavior. For those who grew up in an emotionally abusive environment as a child, there is a real danger of unwittingly perpetuating those childhood patterns in adult relationships. We have found that often a fear of repeating such behavior with children, spouses, or other loved ones is the motivation that propels emotionally abused people into counseling. In horror, they see themselves doing as an adult the very thing they hated as a child. This shock is enough to bring about recognition of the dysfunction of their relationships and a desire to pursue healthy definitions of love.

Emotional abuse is a systematic assault on another person's sense of self. The damage done to that person is pervasive and persistent. When the sense of self is decimated, the person can look to other people to provide emotional security and identity. The damage done can also contribute to the traits of a dependent personality. Consider again dependent personality traits. A dependent person:

- has difficulty making everyday decisions without an excessive amount of advice and reassurance from others
- needs others to assume responsibility for many major areas of life[2]
- has difficulty expressing disagreement with others because of fear of losing their support or approval
- struggles to start projects or do things because of a lack of trust in personal judgment or abilities
- goes to excessive lengths to obtain nurture and support from others, to the point of volunteering to do things they would rather not do
- feels anxious or distressed when alone out of fear they won't be able to handle what might happen on their own
- urgently seeks another relationship as a source of care and support when a close relationship ends
- feels better about focusing attention on solving the problems of others than on solving personal issues
- puts the needs of others above their own needs, even if they are really hurting or resentful
- takes on the responsibility of meeting the needs of others, even if unasked or if those needs are hurtful, difficult, or even impossible
- considers self to be responsible when bad things happen, even outside events and circumstances
- feels responsible for fulfilling the expectations of others and a failure if that doesn't happen
- is aware of the needs and feelings of others but unsure of personal needs and feelings

- considers the opinions and feelings of others as greater in value than their own
- has a high need for validation and approval from others
- adapts behavior and even physical appearance to the desires of others
- is unable to create or defend personal boundaries because of fear of rejection
- is unfamiliar with or unsure of appropriate boundaries for intimacy
- attempts to manipulate others and situations in order to maintain relationships
- has difficulty accepting challenging or disturbing truths about self or others out of a need to maintain the status quo

Are you seeing the connection between the two lists? Emotional abuse destroys a sense of self. When a sense of self is destroyed, the person looks to others to provide a structure for self. Giving another person the authority to define who you were, who you are, and who you want to be is to give that person tremendous power over you. When anything or anyone holds that much power over you, the potential for abuse exists. Keep those characteristics in mind as you read the next two lists from my (Dr. Gregg's) book on emotional abuse. To the original list, we've added some comments about emotional abuse and relationship dependency.

Negative Effects of Emotional Abuse on Self

- *Low self-esteem*. Emotional abuse robs a person of a healthy sense of self, creating a deficit in the ability to think positively about self—a deficit the person seeks to fill through relationships with others.

- *Lack of self-confidence.* Emotional abuse undercuts a person's belief in their ability to accomplish tasks, goals, and dreams, creating a condition in which others are given the power to dictate those tasks, goals, and dreams.

- *Transfer of needs.* Emotional abuse removes a person's sense of trust in their ability to care for self, necessitating a transfer of needs from that person to another person.

- *Acting out sexually.* Emotional abuse destroys a person's belief that they are capable and worthy of love. Without a sense of worth or value, the person will exchange sexual behavior for attention and validation.

- *Loneliness.* Emotional abuse drains a person of the capacity to create and maintain healthy, uplifting relationships, resulting in personal isolation, despair, and loneliness, which feed the cycle of relationship dependency.

- *Failure syndrome.* Emotional abuse convinces a person that they are not capable and that discovery of those failings could happen at any time, leading to humiliation and rejection. To avoid surprise discovery, the emotionally abused person will sometimes create failure, including self-sabotaging relationships, in an attempt to orchestrate and control the discovery.

- *Perfectionism.* Emotional abuse sets an impossible standard for love and acceptance, a bar the person attempts to reach time and time again, with inevitable failure acting to reinforce the person's sense of unworthiness and need to achieve perfection to gain approval.

Perfectionism undercuts the conditions necessary for a healthy relationship.

- *Unrealistic guilt.* Emotional abuse heaps the weight of another's disappointment, anger, and rage onto the back of an innocent person. Over time, this guilt becomes an accustomed weight, and the person fails to recognize the drag this weight causes in relationships.

- *Crisis oriented.* Emotional abuse is a roller coaster of emotional onslaughts and manufactured crises. This adrenaline-pumping blitzkrieg becomes the established norm, and its absence creates uncertainty, fear, and anxiety. Relationships fail when others refuse to go along on such an up-and-down, twisting-and-turning ride.

- *Unresolved anger and resentment.* Emotional abuse is unfair. For most people who are attacked through emotional abuse, a part of them recognizes the unfairness of the treatment, resulting in anger and resentment. However, because of the persistent pattern of abuse, the person does not have an opportunity to express the anger or resentment, so they remain bottled up and unresolved, festering and poisoning self and other relationships.

We are sure you can see how these characteristics merge and intertwine. Next, let's look at the negative effects of emotional abuse on relationships. Again, this list comes from my (Dr. Gregg's) book on emotional abuse, with added commentary.

▪ Negative Effects of Emotional Abuse on Relationships

- *Distortion of what is normal, with negative consequences to all relationships.* Emotional abuse resets normal with unhealthy and dysfunctional parameters. When seeking a "normal" relationship, an emotionally abused person ends up looking in all the wrong places.

- *Undercutting of a strong and healthy sense of self.* We've gone over this concept as an integral part of the disruptive pattern of relationship dependency. A healthy sense of self is integral to all relationships. When it is absent, a relationship suffers.

- *Establishment of a potential for emotional abuse in future relationships.* Emotional abuse sets up a swirling vortex of emotions and actions with the power to grab and negatively affect future relationships.

- *Difficulty with intimacy.* Intimacy requires trust, belief, and respect, all of which are systematically damaged or destroyed by emotional abuse. Without this positive foundation, healthy intimacy is at a severe disadvantage.

- *Caution, fear, and suspicion in relationships.* When the context for relationships is emotional abuse, relationships themselves become suspect and risky.

- *Perfectionism.* Perfectionism is not toxic to just one person in a relationship. The toxicity from perfectionism pollutes all parties in the relationship. The emotionally abused person feels they must be perfect to be loved but also resents having such a tremendous burden placed on them.

- *Feelings of abandonment.* A person living daily with another person can, nonetheless, be abandoned. When the other person is an emotional abuser, that person has abandoned their responsibility to cherish, accept, nurture, protect, and guide the other person. Constantly

seeking after what is never provided creates a vicious
cycle of hope dashed and disappointment.

- *Emotional triggers of fear, guilt, and anger.* Emotional
  abuse heightens a person's negative emotions. Fear,
  guilt, and anger are constantly on the surface, ready
  to be triggered by the slightest touch, intentional or
  unintentional. An emotionally unstable person contributes to an emotionally unstable relationship.

- *Hypersensitivity.* Emotional abuse rubs a person's emotional skin raw, creating a situation of hypersensitivity
  and putting undue pressure on relationships.

- *Tension and confusion in current relationships, including work relationships.* People who are emotionally
  abused experience tension and confusion across the
  spectrum of relationships, not only in family relationships. Any relationship that might speak into the value
  or worth of the person is negatively affected by fear,
  anger, and doubt. Friendships, work relationships, and
  associations all become complicated because of the effects of emotional abuse.

- *Rejection of authority or need for controlling authority
  figures.* People respond to emotional abuse in a variety of ways, including both rejecting authority of any
  kind and desiring to substitute one controlling figure
  for another. In addition, the person may choose to become their own surrogate authority figure, meting out
  learned harsh judgment to self and others as a way
  to re-create "normalcy." Relationships require mutual
  understanding and acceptance, which cannot be given
  in these situations.

- *Cycling the pattern of abuse with one's own children.* Emotional abuse sets up a pattern of behavior that can overtake and inundate successive generations, especially when that abuse remains unchallenged.

- *Codependency.* This was one entry in a very long list that, over the years, we have both come to realize is significant and underrecognized, contributing to the book you now have in your hands.

- *Unhealthy desire to be needed.* Emotional abuse dangles the carrot of acceptance constantly out of reach, propelling the person to greater and greater effort to gain approval. This pattern of people pleasing leads to an unhealthy desire to be perceived as needed and necessary by others, making the person a target for those who would take advantage.

- *Isolation from others.* Emotional abuse creates an atmosphere of suspicion, distrust, and anxiety in relationships that can cause a person to conclude after successive relationship failures that a lack of relationships is the only safe alternative. Yet without a sense of self, the person continues to be drawn into relationships that create such fear.

- *Inappropriate coping activities, such as television, internet, gaming, or food.* Emotional abuse produces a cavalcade of negative emotions, promoting a variety of self-soothing and self-numbing activities that can become addictive on their own and can exist in competition with relationships.

- *Excessive compliance or passivity.* There comes a point when a person is so beaten down emotionally that they lose the will to fight for self and capitulate to the control of others.

Emotional abuse, especially in childhood, creates the conditions for dependency traits in adulthood. These dependency traits infiltrate and influence the creation and maintenance of relationships. The adult tries time and time again—either within a single relationship or through multiple relationships—to re-create conditions of childhood that were mistakenly or manipulatively labeled as necessary, at best, or loving, at worst.

The Point of Realization

Drew stopped as he walked past Caleb's room, straining to hear if Caleb was playing one of his video games with the sound turned down. Drew's anger, still simmering close to the surface, was ready to blow if Caleb was being disobedient. Listening intently, Drew could hear muffled sounds coming from inside the room. With a shock, Drew realized those muffled sounds were his son crying. He heard his son punching, probably his pillow, and saying over and over again, "You're so stupid! You're so stupid!" Instantly, Drew was transported back almost twenty-five years to his own room, to his own frustration, to his own realization that he just wasn't as smart as he needed to be. Now it was happening all over again with Caleb. How had he let this happen? How had he made his son feel so bad about himself? He just wanted Caleb to do better than he had at his age, yet he'd made his son feel worse.

There comes a point in a person's life when that person says, "Enough." Each person needs to decide where that point is. Once that point is reached, the person is ready to commit to the kind of changes necessary to remake life and relationships. Sometimes that point is reached by looking into a mirror. Sometimes that point is reached by looking into the face of another. Always that point is reached when a person realizes there is more to love than what they experienced.

When a person comes to understand that there is more to love than what they experienced, this knowledge can be devastating. Acknowledging a past in which emotional abuse was present means acknowledging a damaged past. We have seen adults cling desperately to the illusion of a loving childhood with excuses such as, "It wasn't so bad," "He was only trying to help," "She just didn't know any better," or "I've gotten over it."

One of the core traits of a dependent personality is difficulty accepting challenging or disturbing truths about self or others out of a need to maintain the status quo. To cover over the harsh reality of an emotionally abusive past, the person seeks to redefine the emotionally abusive behavior as loving and necessary. The only way to justify the necessity for such harsh behavior toward self by another is to agree through self-condemnation. In that warped view of childhood, a loving parent was still possible, if only the child had been good enough. The fault, then, lies with the child, and accepting fault keeps the dream of a loving parent alive.

This is the sliver of hope that emotionally abused children cling to. To finally admit, as an adult, that there was nothing they could have done to win that parent's love or acceptance is to crush that fragile sliver of hope. Emotionally abused people often must believe love was a possibility then in order to believe that love is a possibility now.

That fragile sliver of hope may be crushed by an acknowledgment of emotional abuse, but hope need not be completely lost. By giving up the illusion and accepting the truth, you can finally turn your energy toward learning to live with that truth. By giving up promoting the lie, you can choose to examine all the facets of the truth. The truth may be you had a parent or other person who was incapable of truly loving you, but that is not the whole truth. Those earthly people may have fallen short, but God does not. You have a loving Father who has always looked at you with love and accepts you for who you are. There may be people who did not have the capacity to truly love or accept you for who you are, but God does. Because he does, you can learn how too.

Connection Point

Each of us is a compilation of our experiences, both good and bad. Over the years, we have developed a way of looking at ourselves that comes, in large part, from how others view us, both good and bad. Emotional abuse manufactures and accentuates the bad while twisting and sabotaging the good. A primary way emotional abuse works is through the messages conveyed through actions, attitudes, and behaviors.

Earlier, we listed the signs of emotional abuse. In this section, we'd like you to look at them and think about whether or not they have been present in your life. As you do so, search for prevalent themes or messages you remember growing up, communicated to you through actions, attitudes, or behaviors. While emotional abuse is certainly a pattern of behavior, be aware that you may also remember a particular incident of great impact on your sense of self. The pattern of emotional abuse can be so prevalent that it runs in the background of life until a specific instance uncovers its negativity with great force. Such a specific instance is the exclamation point to an underlying message. Think back and watch for the patterns, but also be aware that you may have pivotal memories of lasting impact.

As you look over this list again, rate the impact on your life of each one on a scale of 1 to 5, with 1 representing no impact and 5 representing major impact.

As you were growing up, did you experience actions, attitudes, or behaviors in which another person:

- intentionally made you feel worthless
- put the blame for another's mistakes on you
- minimized or dismissed your point of view
- threatened or hinted at physical or sexual abuse
- went into fits of rage and intense anger toward you
- failed to fulfill commitments or promises made or implied to you
- intentionally lied to you to avoid responsibility for the truth
- refused to acknowledge your feelings
- verbally or physically humiliated you through inappropriate gestures, comments, or jokes
- used shame or guilt to manipulate your actions
- did not allow you to articulate your feelings
- denied you access to your personal possessions or pets
- withheld appropriate financial resources
- refused to communicate with you through variations of the silent treatment

- displayed extreme ranges of mood, creating uncertainty and fear
- made conditional agreements in which the conditions kept changing so they could avoid fulfilling the agreement
- used a hostile or sarcastic tone of voice with you
- was critical of your actions, attitudes, or behaviors
- viewed you as a part of their own personality as opposed to a person with your own thoughts, feelings, and opinions
- belittled, humiliated, marginalized, and/or ignored you

For each of these with a 3 or above, name the person who treated you this way. You may be resistant to commit to such a designation. If so, write down why it is difficult for you to name that person. Look over how many times that person appears next to one of these signs of emotional abuse. The more times the name appears, the more influence that person has had on your view of yourself, life, hope, and future. Your vision has been shaped by that person, and it may be time for you to identify that vision and tell yourself, "Enough." Saying enough is an ending, but it is also a beginning—a new beginning for yourself, for those you love in the present, and for those you will love in the future.

6

How Does Spiritual Abuse Contribute to Relationship Dependency?

We are Christian counselors, and many of the people we have worked with over the years have also been Christians or people of faith. These individuals have come to us for help and guidance, seeking a treatment environment in which faith is accepted and integrated into care. They have sought a place to express and strengthen their faith, understanding faith to be a valuable resource in recovery. Other people have come to a deeper understanding of and connection to their faith as a part of their journey toward healing and restoration. We know and have seen the power of spirituality in long-term recovery.

Sadly, we have also seen the power of spirituality gone wrong in the lives of those we've counseled. Instead of seeing

God as a loving, merciful Father, some people have an image of God as a harsh, unfeeling tyrant. Instead of God's words being a balm for the hurts and pains of this world, his words have been used as a biblical bludgeon. Instead of having a God who knows them by name and accepts them, these people have an image of a God who rejects them as flawed, damaged, and unlovable. We do not believe these devastatingly negative portraits of God are the truth. When these false portraits of a vengeful, unloving, condemning, distant, and disgusted super being are used, the result is a type of spiritual abuse. Spiritual abuse is a very real experience for some people who have been told that God condemns them. If you believe you are forever condemned, how can you find hope?

■ What Is Spiritual Abuse?

In the last chapter, we talked about how emotional abuse takes lies and parades those lies as the truth to manipulate and control. Spiritual abuse is similar. Spiritual abuse happens when lies are told as if those lies are the truth of God. Spiritual abuse is used as a way to manipulate and control. Spiritual abuse is usurping divine authority in order to promote self, which is the opposite of what God does. God uses his divine authority and nature to promote others from a position of love, grace, and mercy.

Who would misuse the words and character of God to perpetrate such a damaging falsehood? Tragically, some people do within the context of relationships. God, as the author of relationships, can be misrepresented and misquoted by those who seek to use relationships for power and control. When a person twists the truth of God to promote self, that person gains tremendous power over others. If a person hides under a religious mantle, then to question that person's actions is to question God.

How is spiritual abuse manifested within relationships? When God, the Bible, and/or faith is used to weaken or destroy a person's sense of self, spiritual abuse is present. The motivation behind the use of religion in this situation is not spiritual enlightenment but spiritual enslavement. When the spiritual abuser becomes the final arbiter for God's will, then only by remaining in relationship with that person can the "truth" be known. In contrast, being out of relationship with that person becomes the same as leaving the "truth."

Spiritual abuse happens any time a person usurps the power and authority of God to harm another person or to promote self at the expense of another. Extreme examples of spiritual abuse include Jonestown in Guyana (1978) and Waco in Texas (1993). In these rare and extreme cases, spiritual abuse resulted in physical death. More prevalent, in our experience, is when spiritual abuse results in spiritual death. When spiritual abuse is present, hope dies, faith is starved, trust is annihilated, and self is strangled.

As we have said, at the root of dependency is an inability to be in true relationship with self. When this foundational relationship is damaged, other relationships are compromised. Misusing God's Word, using religion as a way to scrape off a person's sense of self, is a way for an abuser to create dependency. When the abuser takes on the equivalence of God, disobedience and doubt become defined as sin, with here-and-now as well as eternal consequences.

The misuse of God's Word and of his nature is an ancient practice. Throughout history, there have been those who have claimed to speak for God but were only speaking for themselves. God tells Jeremiah, "I did not send these prophets, yet they have run with their message; I did not speak to them, yet they have prophesied" (Jer. 23:21). People today are still running with their own messages, pretending to be from God, causing damage and harm.

As a disclaimer, neither of us believes it is possible to completely understand every nuance of Scripture or to know at each moment what the will of God is for all things. If we could, we would be like God, omniscient or all-knowing.

But spiritual abuse is not the unintentional misunderstanding of a spiritual truth. Spiritual abuse is the intentional misrepresentation of a spiritual truth for unspiritual reasons, such as greed, manipulation, injustice, hatred, or spite. Spiritual abuse is not a lack of knowledge. Spiritual abuse is using knowledge not to enlighten but to control, which is the opposite of what God does. God gives people truth so they can make a choice; spiritual abusers give people lies so they can take away those choices. Within relationships, spiritual abuse happens when one person misrepresents the truth in order to control and create dependency in another person.

As we have worked with people struggling with relationship dependency issues, we've heard spiritual falsehoods quoted back to us as the truth. Sometimes people come to suspect that what they've been told about God isn't true. Yet because of spiritual battering, they don't believe in their own ability to come to an independent knowledge of the truth. Caught between knowing something isn't right but not trusting themselves to come to the truth, they can become angry—at themselves, others, and God.

110

One of the most challenging tasks of a Christian counselor is to untangle those spiritual falsehoods from a person's faith in God because, have no doubt, some people have developed a deeply entrenched faith in their own unworthiness, their own unlovable nature, and their own hopelessness that is tightly bound to their belief in God. They have bound a belief in an all-powerful God with a surety of their own worthlessness. We must gently peel away the untruths they've been taught and help them to discover the truth from the Source. Sometimes we must first convince them that they have the capacity to understand the truth of God's Word without someone else, including us, acting as their filter.

To confront lies with truth, it is vital to go back to the very words of God that were used to spiritually bludgeon and to look at those words afresh through the lens of love and grace. Contemplating a different interpretation, a different viewpoint, than the one they received provides a personal connection between them and God. This also helps them to regain trust in their ability to decide, for themselves, what God is saying to them and why.

The Misuse of Scripture in Spiritual Abuse

To demonstrate how spiritual abuse works, we have outlined the five passages of Scripture we have seen most misused during our years of counseling. We outline how we have seen each misused and then seek to present an alternative perspective based on our own understanding of God. We do not demand that you agree with our understanding; we ask only that you consider that the way you've been taught to view God may deserve another look.

■ ■ ■

Do nothing out of selfish ambition or vain conceit. Rather, in humility value others above yourselves. (Phil. 2:3)

If you are a Christian who struggles with dependency issues, this Scripture passage can be difficult for you to understand (along with Rom. 12:10). You already doubt yourself and consider other people better than you. When you read these words, you may hear an echo of, "You are not special, and if you think you are, then you are selfish and vain. God says other people are better than you."

We don't believe this passage was written to belittle, minimize, or diminish you. We don't believe this is a passage about who you are as a person. Instead, we believe this passage speaks about what you do. This is a passage that speaks about motivations. This passage instructs people to examine the heart, the motives, behind their actions. Actions that are done because of selfish ambition and vain conceit are to be avoided. Prideful selfishness destroys relationships because one person is elevated by marginalizing another.

This passage in Philippians also does not say that other people are better than you. Instead, this passage recommends that you consider adopting a specific position when dealing with other people. First, watch your own motives for selfishness and vanity; second, when possible, defer to others out of love. But what are the motives of those who use this passage to their own advantage, to control others and force subservience? Those motives spring from the very attitudes and actions warned about in the passage—selfish ambition and vain conceit. This passage speaks specifically against the very way it is used by the spiritually abusive.

Using this Scripture passage to tell a person they are not special is selfish and vain. Only those who seek to hijack and dispense "specialness" would attempt to withhold that knowledge from others. You are special according to God. He loves you and sent Jesus to die for you. Some of you will counter this assertion by saying that God doesn't really love you, that he loves the whole world, which is different. Yes, you are a part of the larger world he loves. However, we firmly believe that if there had been just one person who needed the saving grace of God, just one and not the whole world, Jesus would still have gone to the cross for that one. As we understand the nature of God's love, we understand that one person is me (Dr. Gregg), that one person is me (Dr. Tim), and that one person is you.

■ ■ ■

Love is patient, love is kind. It does not envy, it does not boast, it is not proud. It does not dishonor others, it is not self-seeking, it is not easily angered, it keeps no record of wrongs. Love does not delight in evil but rejoices with the truth. It always protects, always trusts, always hopes, always perseveres. (1 Cor. 13:4–7)

We used this passage in the chapter on emotional abuse to contrast the characteristics of love with abuse. This description of love is one of the most beautiful, affirming, and encouraging passages of Scripture. Because God is love, this passage speaks directly to God's nature. We believe love is God's essential nature.

Cruelly, some take this passage of Scripture not as an explanation of the heart of God but as a list of tasks that must be carried out perfectly in order to be loving. These words on love are used as a spiritual club to religiously whack the imperfect for every failure to perform. Of course, those who use this passage to abuse others make themselves the judge of what behavior constitutes patience, kindness, envy, boasting, pride, etc. Instead of looking to God for definitions, these people substitute themselves and use their own definitions to manipulate, control, belittle, and demean others. We have seen this passage on love used in a most unloving manner, as an impossible standard by which others are judged and condemned.

■ ■ ■

If someone slaps you on one cheek, turn to them the other also. If someone takes your coat, do not withhold your shirt from them. Give to everyone who asks you, and if anyone takes what belongs to you, do not demand it back. (Luke 6:29–30)

Those who misuse this passage interpret it to say that what you have is not your own. To be a Christian, you must allow other people to take what belongs to you. Do you really believe that? Would you allow someone to come into your home and take whatever they want? Of course not! That is called theft. Dependent people become confused over what is theft and what is love because of who does the taking. If a stranger takes something, it's theft. If a family member or friend takes something, it's supposed to be love.

So how do you reconcile these words of Jesus? We believe this passage is part of a larger section on how a person is to deal with an enemy that begins in verse 27 and ends in verse 36. Enemies are those who would hit you and steal from you and demand what you have.

This passage tells you that when you are powerless to stop an enemy, give in and rely on God to make things right. Save yourself in the moment and look to God for resolution. You, however, are not required to remain anyone's punching bag, physically or emotionally.

■ ■ ■

> The wife's body does not belong to her alone but also to her husband. In the same way, the husband's body does not belong to him alone but also to his wife. Do not deprive each other except by mutual consent and for a time, so that you may devote yourselves to prayer. Then come back together again so that Satan will not tempt you because of your lack of self-control. (1 Cor. 7:4–5 NIV 1984)

We have seen this passage of Scripture misunderstood by those who have difficulty with intimacy in dependent relationships. Sadly, this passage has been misused to tell a wife she has no right to her own body. This passage has justified making a wife sexually subservient to whatever her husband wants.

A wife does not give up control of her own body in marriage. The opening sentence of this passage says clearly that a wife's body belongs to her. However, in marriage, her body "does not belong to her alone." This is because she is not alone; she is married. Her body is hers, but her body is also part of the unity of the marriage. The husband's body is also part of the unity of the marriage. The passage says, "in the same way," speaking about the husband's body. The goal of marriage is joint physical submission and unity for the good of the marriage. Turning this passage into the equivalent of scriptural approval for sexual abuse within marriage is spiritual abuse. Relationship guidelines in Scripture are not meant to create dominancy. Rather, relationship guidelines are meant to model the sacrificial love of God and Christ.

■ ■ ■

Children, obey your parents in the Lord, for this is right. (Eph. 6:1)

Too frequently, we have both worked with adults, male and female, who had a warped view of God because of dysfunctional parenting. They had a parent who misused Scripture and spiritual concepts to belittle, demean, and criticize them as a child. These individuals took the difficult and damaging parent they lived with as a child and projected that image onto God. God's image, then, was not his own but was overshadowed by that parental image. When this happens, God does not speak with his own voice; the parental voice becomes God's voice, with all its inherent authority.

When a child is told that God approves of, and even commands, harsh treatment by a spiritually abusive parent, the child is even more convinced of their worthlessness. Scripture is used to destroy the child's sense of self, and that child becomes susceptible to dependency behaviors in every relationship going forward. Convinced of their lack of value, the child will look to others to provide purpose, validation, and approval in relationships. If you were deprived of love, grace, and acceptance as a child, you may desperately seek after them, all the while convinced of being completely unworthy of receiving them. This is the horrific catch-22 of relationship dependency compounded by spiritual abuse.

If you were spiritually abused as a child, you may seek out a familiar religious environment as an adult. Within that religious environment, you may seek to create relationships with others who hold a worldview similar to what you learned growing up. When this worldview is formed in childhood and reinforced in adulthood, you may find it difficult to break the chains of spiritual abuse. We have watched the struggle of those seeking to escape those bonds. We have also seen the liberating truth of the love of God create freedom, forgiveness, love, and acceptance.

◼ The Relationship between Spiritual Abuse and Dependency

The concepts of spiritual abuse are tailor-made for traits of dependency. Below are the dependency traits explained earlier connected with the spiritual misuse and abuse that can contribute to those traits.

Difficulty making everyday decisions without advice and reassurance and needing others to assume responsibility for major areas of life.

Dependency says you are not worthy to make your own decisions. Spiritual abuse can echo that sentiment, reinforcing the idea that you are not worthy to make your own decisions, from major life decisions down to everyday decisions. Spiritual abuse seeks to make you so distrustful of self that you seek out the spiritual abuser to find out how to live your life. Dependency leaves you without a defense against the abuse.

Difficulty disagreeing with others out of fear.

Spiritual abuse makes disagreeing with another person equal to disagreeing with God. Accepting yourself becomes the same as rejecting God. A dependent person is already fearful of disagreement because of real-time consequences. When combined with spiritual abuse, real-time fears are combined with eternal ones.

Struggling to start projects or do things on your own.

Spirituality is not a stagnant, one-time destination. Rather, it should be a personal, continual journey of growth and enlightenment. With spiritual abuse, taking such a journey is forbidden, as the path might lead you away from the influence and control of the abuser.

Doing things you don't want to do to gain approval.

If you will do things you don't want to do to gain earthly approval, you may be even more motivated for heavenly approval. This is a damaging combination for a dependent person who has undergone spiritual abuse. The list of unwanted things you are willing to do can become dangerously long.

Feeling extreme anxiety at the thought of being alone.

Spiritual abuse says that without the approval of others, you are alone and condemned. Only by being in proximity to others, who can vouch for you and provide you with direction and purpose, are you able to have a chance at salvation. If you are separated from those who know better than you, you are lost and cut off from God. Your salvation is tied to other people, so you must be in a relationship. A relationship is safety; being alone is dangerous.

Urgently seeking another relationship when a close relationship ends.

Spiritual abuse seeks to convince you that you are unworthy of God's love. Convinced of this unworthiness, you may attempt to avoid developing a closer relationship with God, sure that he will reject you. Intentionally isolating from God means you may shy away from him during times of emotional distress, such as during the loss of a close relationship. Keeping God at arms' length, you may rob yourself of a divine source of love and comfort.

Focusing attention and effort on solving the problems of others.

Spiritual abuse says that in order to be spiritual and acceptable to God, you must disregard your own problems and seek instead to solve the problems of others. If you are a truly loving person, you will never seek your own good but always seek the good of others. Spiritual abuse agrees with relationship dependency when it says that the only way you can seek to please God is to please other people. Other people, then, become your avenue for redemption.

Putting the needs of others above self.

Spiritual abuse says you are not entitled to your own needs because other people are better than you. You learn to bury your own needs so effectively that you become unsure of what your needs really are. You may become anxious when asked to define them. You would rather spend your energy discerning the needs of others. Because those needs are easier to recognize, they are easier to meet. When meeting the needs of others becomes your main purpose in life, you must have others willing to allow you to meet their needs. Relationships, then, become your priority.

Taking responsibility for the needs of others.

Spiritual abuse says that you are not special. Spiritual abuse says that other people are better than you because you are unworthy and unlovable. The only way to redeem yourself is to devote yourself to those who are better than you, to those anointed by God over you. They have a spiritual right to command you to do whatever they deem necessary. Disobedience toward the person becomes disobedience toward God. Thus, the relationship takes on divine significance. Spiritual abuse emphasizes blame and withholds grace. Meeting the needs of others, then, becomes your penance, and relationships become your avenue for salvation.

Feeling responsible for outside events and circumstances.

Because spiritual abuse emphasizes that you are such a failure and disappointment in life, you become used to accepting responsibility when bad things happen. The only way for you to feel any sense of control is to take responsibility and try to fix things. This tendency to take the blame and try to fix things becomes a pattern lived out within relationships.

Feeling responsible for fulfilling others' expectations.

Spiritual abuse says that your unworthiness always causes you to fall short. In an attempt to prove your worth, you try over and over again to fulfill the expectations of others, no matter what those expectations are. When those expectations are outlandish, you see that as a greater opportunity to prove your worth by meeting them. But because the expectations are so outlandish, you have little chance of actually meeting them. You try; you fail. You try again; you fail again. You keep trying spiritually, and you keep trying relationally.

Recognizing others' needs but unsure of your own.

Spiritual abuse says that to be acceptable to God, you must meet the needs, desires, and expectations of others. Because you do not trust yourself to do this, you must monitor the feelings of others to see if you are succeeding or failing. Salvation is found in reading and adjusting to the feelings of others and doing everything you can to make those feelings good ones. When you make yourself responsible for the happiness of everyone around you, you make yourself responsible for everything that happens around you.

Spiritual abuse says that what you feel is unimportant; only what others feel is important. So you bury your own needs and learn to become adept at ferreting out the needs of others. After a time, you become unsure of what your own needs are. The more your identity is tied to the feelings of others, the less you are anchored to yourself. The less you are anchored to yourself, the more susceptible you are to the vicious cycle of relationship dependency.

Considering the opinions and feelings of others as greater in value than your own.

Dependency can cause you to undervalue your own opinions and feelings and overvalue those of others. Spiritual abusers are often dogmatic, opinionated individuals who are only too happy to batter you with their opinions and feelings. Your opinions and feelings are irrelevant to spiritual abusers, who tap into this dependent tendency, misusing Scripture to further devalue you as a person in order to elevate themselves.

Spiritual abuse says that you are a willful, sinful, disobedient person who has no right to have any good feelings about yourself. Spiritual abuse says that only another, more righteous person can determine if you have any right to feel good about yourself. The only time you can feel good about yourself is when someone else gives you permission. Wanting desperately to feel good about yourself, you seek relationships with others who will give you permission. Often, however, those you choose withhold or barter for that permission.

Having a high need for external validation.

Spiritual abuse confirms the false idea that what others think about you is more important than what you think about you. After all, you are flawed and sinful; therefore, any opinions and feelings you have are also flawed and sinful. As a way to atone for your flawed and sinful self, you seek the approval and validation of others and will do just about anything to get them.

Adapting behavior and appearance to others.

Spiritual abuse says that you are not able to come to decisions and conclusions about what is best for you; you must look to others for the "truth." Because you need others to define you, you must look for others willing to define you. Those willing to define you are often those most willing to be harsh, judgmental, and critical. Since these are the very attitudes you are familiar with, you don't question their negative conclusions and seek to do what you are told. Being told what to do, how to act, even what to wear gives you structure and a way to gain approval. Finding and maintaining such directive relationships become vital to the framework of your life.

Being unable to create, maintain, or defend appropriate boundaries.

Spiritual abuse says that you have no right to personal boundaries; you must adhere to the boundaries set in place by others who are more knowledgeable and righteous than you. If you attempt to set personal boundaries at odds with another, you must give in to that other person. Even the concept of personal boundaries is sinful and willful because people should be able to take what is yours, and you must not demand it back; to do so is against God's will. Speaking up for yourself is arrogant and unscriptural.

Being unfamiliar with healthy intimacy.

Spiritual abuse says that, if you are a married woman, you belong to your husband; you are not your own. You are to do whatever is necessary to meet the needs and desires of your husband, including sexual needs. In order to be submissive to your husband, who is in authority over you, you must submit to his sexual control over you.

For either gender, when you place low value on yourself and high value on others, the mutual respect and love necessary for healthy intimacy are damaged. Sexual intimacy is a gift one person, in love, gives to another. However, when you do not value yourself, you do not see yourself as capable of giving anything but obedience and submission. Intimacy, then, becomes a duty, a task to be performed.

Trying to manipulate and control people and situations to create safety.

Spiritual abuse says that you are responsible for the happiness of others and that failure to make them happy is a sin. So you commit to working as hard as you can to meet the needs of others. When they are difficult or impossible to meet, you attempt to control the other people to force a necessary outcome. You try to manipulate and control people and circumstances in order to create more safety.

Denying and avoiding reality.

Spiritual abuse says that failure has eternal consequences. Spiritual abuse says that when you have failed the other person, you have failed God. You have been taught that failing God leads to eternal damnation. Therefore, failure is not an option. In order to function, you must continue to believe that success, that redemption, is possible, so you cling to the view that success is still possible, regardless of the results.

■ ■ ■

The consequences of spiritual abuse flow easily into the consequences of relationship dependency. Spiritual abuse creates dependency because it destroys the inner core of self. If you do not know who you are, how can you truly connect with God? In our experience, spiritually abused people can be like wounded puppies, desperate to get inside the master's house, to be fed and warmed, but terrified of what might happen once the door opens.

We have also found that once spiritually abused people begin to recognize themselves and God and begin to draw near to him in confidence, amazing healing happens. Instead of being fearful of a vengeful God, they begin to draw near to the open arms of a loving Father. Instead of seeing themselves through the eyes of their spiritual abuser, they begin to see themselves through the eyes of a merciful Savior. Instead of believing themselves incapable of understanding God, they begin to trust in God's ability to reveal himself to them. When God is allowed to speak for himself, spiritual renewal and transformation become possible.

Connection Point

This chapter has been devoted to countering spiritual abuse and some of the misuse of Scripture and spiritual concepts we've seen through our years of counseling. We have found that even those who did not grow up in a faith community can be victims of spiritual abuse. Those who attend or have attended church are not the only people who misuse spiritual concepts. Just as Satan masquerades as an angel of light, so do others, others who have never stepped inside a church. God's name and character can be misused by people who have nothing to do with a church or faith community.

For this exercise, we'd like you to consider what you know about God, however you define God.

1. What did you believe about God as a child?
2. What are the sources of those childhood beliefs?
3. What do you believe about God now?
4. How did you come to any new ideas on your own? Was it through your own life experience, through study, or did someone tell them to you?

We believe people are spiritual beings and this life is not the end. We believe people have a capacity for faith, whether it is faith based on hope or faith based on despair. Those most fearful of God often deal with that fear by refusing to think about him. If this is true of you, now is the time to evaluate what you believe about God and about yourself as you relate to God.

To counter a spiritual untruth, you first need to uncover it. God is so much bigger than we can possibly comprehend. If God has been presented to you in a small, cramped, and locked box full of negativity, judgment, and condemnation, it's time for you to get a different—and much bigger—box.

7

What Is the Role of the Brain in Relationship Dependency?

Karen was euphoric. Everything with Mark was going so well. For what seemed like the twentieth time during the past hour, she picked up her cell phone and reread the short text: "Miss u see u tonite xo." Karen could hardly wait. Whenever she thought of seeing Mark in just a few short hours, she could feel her heart and breathing speed up. Her stomach got that swooping feeling, and she felt so pent up that staying seated at her desk was impossible. Good thing her supervisor was at a conference, because Karen's productivity today was registering in the negative range. All she wanted to do was think about Mark and go over their short courtship. The hours could not pass quickly enough until she could be with him again. Mark was perfect, everything she could want.

There is a reason why a version of the scenario above has been repeated in innumerable love stories. There is magic when something is able to transform your world. There is also power when something is able to transform your world. Love has been called magic, but love is really the power to create change, emotional and physiological change. One thing is for sure—love is affective.

The affective nature of love is what has inspired artistic expression for millennia. Much of that artistic expression has centered on the more extreme physiological effects of being in love. Your heart pounds; your breathing speeds up; your thoughts continually return to the object of your affection. A word, a look (nowadays a text) can bring you from the height of ecstasy to the valley of despair and back again. You're in love, and there's nothing quite like it.

■ ■ ■

Glancing at the clock, Karen wondered if it would be wrong to text Mark again. Would that be too much? Would he think she was obsessive? Was she obsessive? The way she felt about Mark seemed that way to Karen, but she didn't care. All she cared about was how amazingly good he made her feel. Karen had felt bad for too long and never wanted to go back there. As she thought about the times before, Karen experienced a jolt of fear, enough to deflate her euphoria. She did not want to mess up this relationship with Mark, so she had to be very careful; she had to do everything just right. Karen knew she could mess up a relationship; she had before. Her dating clock was ticking, and she desperately wanted this relationship with Mark to work. He was perfect for her, and Karen's job was to make sure she was perfect for him.

Love and Addiction

Being in love, finding that perfect someone, has been compared to winning the lottery. In our experience, that analogy isn't far off. A person newly in love can react the same way a gambler feels after making that big win. A person newly in love can experience a chemical jolt, akin to a drug hit. "Intense passionate love uses the same system of the brain that gets activated when a person becomes addicted to drugs," said Dr. Arthur Aron, a psychologist at the New York State University at Stony Brook, in a *Huffington Post* story about a research study about people in love.[1] "You can feel happy when you're in love, but you can also feel anxious," said Aron's coauthor, Lucy Brown, a neuroscientist at Albert Einstein College of Medicine in New York. "The other person becomes a goal in life, essentially a prize."[2]

Love can be like the hit of a drug or the high of a win, both activities that can lead to addiction. The link between love and addiction is gaining acceptance. In a study with the rather wordy title "The Behavioral, Anatomical, and Pharmacological Parallels between Social Attachment, Love, and Addiction," the authors conclude that "a significant overlap exists" between the physiological effects of love and addiction. "Social addiction may be understood as a behavioral addiction, whereby the subject becomes addicted to another individual and the cues that predict social reward."[3] The relationships studied included both romantic relationships and parent-child relationships, with the authors coining the term "social addiction" to describe the unhealthy relationships. In our view, social addiction is another term for relationship dependency.

This we know: a dependent person has an intense emotional need to be in a relationship with another person; while in that relationship, there are physiological impacts on body chemistry. Being in a relationship triggers the brain's reward center, just like a hit of a drug. Being out of a relationship triggers feelings of depression and anxiety. Emotional responses, then, become intertwined with physical responses, each supporting the other, creating a powerful pull toward relationship. A relationship becomes the goal—the prize—that allows the person to feel good and reduce pain. Is it any wonder you may succumb to relationship dependency with such a powerful mix?

Understanding how addiction happens has been the subject of research for a number of years, starting primarily with alcohol and drug addiction and moving on to behavioral or process addictions, such as gambling and shopping. Only recently has research been undertaken to show how physical addiction can interact with social addiction or, as we call it, relationship dependency.

◾ Addiction and the Brain

Much of this research is technical and the medical language unfamiliar, but we'll attempt to summarize it in layman's terms. In essence, the brain has a reward center within the limbic system. The limbic system is the control center for emotional responses and controls the release of a chemical substance produced by the body called dopamine.

Dopamine is called a neurotransmitter because it allows signals to transmit from one nerve ending to another in the brain. Dopamine makes us feel good, even euphoric. Certain drugs produce a heightened release of dopamine, flooding the brain with an abnormal amount of this feel-good substance.

However, once the brain experiences this wash of dopamine, it attempts to balance itself, shutting off dopamine production and creating the "low" or the "crash" that comes after a "high." Prolonged overstimulation of dopamine through drugs results in a suppression of the limbic system's natural ability to produce dopamine. The brain can no longer produce that feel-good effect on its own. The person becomes physically addicted and, in order to feel good again, must take more and more of the drug.

Alcohol and drugs can trigger the brain to produce artificially high levels of dopamine. Behavioral addictions can also create conditions in which dopamine is produced. The brain can become trained to release dopamine at the pleasure received from activities such as shopping or gambling.

Behavioral addictions intersect with relationship dependency. Outside substances can create a pleasure response in the brain, but so can personal choices. Research has shown that "enhancing the effects of dopamine influences how people make life choices by affecting expectations of pleasure."[4] If you are a dependent person, you have a specific definition of what is pleasurable in relationships for you. Your definition of what is pleasurable can control the release of dopamine within your limbic system. Your behaviors train your brain to recognize pleasure and release dopamine. As one researcher said in a study about the long-term effects of pathological gambling on the brain, "It's not about the brain being addicted to a substance, it's about the brain being addicted to its own chemistry."[5]

Relationship dependency is about the brain being addicted to its own chemistry. As a dependent person, you determine which conditions are safe, which conditions are right, and which conditions are pleasurable. When these predetermined conditions are met, your pleasure center is activated, dopamine is released, and all is right with your world.

■ ■ ■

Sarah's question brought a blush and a rush of pleasure to Karen. Sarah had asked how things were going with Mark. She'd seen Mark pick Karen up from work earlier in the week and was interested to know about this new man in her life. Karen was quick to enumerate Mark's amazing qualities, barely stopping long enough to take a breath. At that, Sarah started laughing, shaking her head and commenting on how Karen had done it again. When Karen asked what she'd done again, Sarah responded, "Why, fall in love, of course!"

Brain Chemistry and Relationship Dependency

Just as we have the ability to determine what situations cause us pleasure, we also have the ability to determine what situations cause us distress. Our determinations of distress can be fairly routine, such as a fear of the dark or falling a great distance or a perceived risk of injury. Yet within those situations is a continuum of tolerance.

For example, with a fear of the dark, some people experience only a mild sense of alertness in the dark. If they fear anything, it's running into something they can't see. However, others undergo heart-pounding, paralyzing fear and disorientation, convinced being in the dark spells imminent danger. Some people become terrified of getting near the edge of a precipice, while others are able to fling themselves over that edge secured only by a bungee cord. For some, the circumstances that spell disaster include traveling over a bridge or flying in a plane or being in the same space as a spider. Our experiences in life help us determine pleasure and where we land on the continuum of distress, training our brain how to respond in each successive situation.

If you are terrified of the dark, you have, in all probability, an actual basis for that fear. Perhaps you had a traumatic experience in the dark. Perhaps you were told you should be afraid of the dark or witnessed an influential person expressing fear of the dark. If you are terrified of heights, you probably experienced some trauma or fright in which heights were involved. If you feel imminent danger concerning bridges or planes or spiders, a connection was made somewhere in your past. When you have predetermined that those experiences are distressing, even anticipating them creates distress. A great deal of your energy, then, is devoted to avoiding those distressing circumstances.

Relationship dependency, as a behavioral process, is an avenue not only for experiencing pleasure but also for avoiding distress. Unfortunately, there may come a point when the pleasure, the euphoria, wears off; the honeymoon is over. The body's ability to keep producing dopamine at heightened levels is compromised. Dopamine suppression can be caused by an overactive and fatigued limbic system. Withdrawal happens; depression sets in because dopamine production is suppressed. Other symptoms of a suppressed dopamine response are anxiety and irritability.[6] Not only does the euphoria evaporate but anxiety and irritability also take up residence. Emotional pain is again experienced, creating the need for more relief.

There is a definitive pattern to addiction that encompasses the mind and the body. This pattern is similar to the cycle of relationship dependency we outlined in chapter 3. We believe relationship dependency and other addictive cycles have similarities because the brain chemistry involved in each is similar. Someone who is chemically addicted uses an outside substance to alter brain chemistry. A dependent person alters their brain through the associations of pleasure and distress within relationships.

■ ■ ■

Karen quickly ran up the back stairs, anxious to avoid Sarah. Sarah asked incessantly about Mark and how the relationship was going and what they were doing and where they were headed. At first, Karen was happy to share, to revel in her relationship with Mark along with Sarah, who seemed as excited as Karen was. But now things weren't going so well. Mark was becoming increasingly distant. The things he used to like he didn't seem to like as much anymore. Just this past week, he'd actually gotten upset that she'd made him dinner on Tuesday, saying he'd told her he'd be watching the game with his brother that night. He accused her of always doing that—not paying attention to what he told her and planning her own activities instead. All the work she had put into dinner didn't seem to matter to him; he had gone to watch the game with his brother, even though she'd offered to bring the meal to his house. The thought of Mark doing things and having fun without her was unsettling. She wanted to do everything with him and desperately wanted him to feel the same way. He should feel the same way. Why didn't he?

■ ■ ■

Every human relationship has ups and downs because people do not stay on an even keel at all times. That is impossible. However, in relationship dependency, as in other types of addictions, the ups and the downs of life become artificially steep. In substance abuse, the effect of the substance on the limbic system and dopamine production creates drug-enhanced highs and system-suppressed lows. With relationship dependency, the stability of the relationship is compromised by the person's dependency traits, as we discussed earlier. Instability in the relationship becomes as assured as the house winning in a gambling addiction. The dependent person sets up conditions for pleasure that are impossible to maintain, guaranteeing failure and the distress that accompanies those failures.

If you struggle with dependency issues in relationships, you may jump to dire conclusions when a relationship hits a rough patch. A forgotten activity becomes a metaphoric slap in the face. An offhand comment becomes the prelude to a breakup. A trivial difference of opinion becomes proof the person is preparing to leave. Just as you determine the conditions that create pleasure, you also determine the conditions that constitute disaster. When disaster seems imminent and assured, your behaviors may escalate and you may feel yourself spinning out of control. You may find yourself losing the relationship and returning to emotional and even physical pain.

■ ■ ■

It was never going to happen; Karen was convinced of it. Mark had been her last chance. Now he was gone. Her chance at love was gone. Her life was gone. How could this have happened again? What was wrong with her? Why did she keep picking the wrong people? When was this going to stop? Karen was so tired. She was tired and defeated and almost without hope. All she wanted was just one person who could love her. After all, weren't there seven billion people in the world? There had to be someone out there for her. There had to be! Maybe she should ask Sarah if she knew someone.

Retraining Your Brain

When an emotional imperative becomes a physical compulsion, the desire to find relief can be overwhelming. In relationship dependency, the brain in the present has been trained to respond to certain conditions by the past. Because of ingrained dependency traits and past experiences, you have written your own list of what creates pleasure for you and what creates distress. At first, your mind was in charge, but over the years your body has become highly influential. You find yourself in the backseat of your own life and responses.

You have trained your body how to respond, and now it's reacting in the way it's been trained, even if you want to feel something different. The silver lining in this scenario is that you can retrain your body to react in a different way. Because we are conscious, thinking creatures and not merely reactive, instinctive creatures, we have the ability to change the way we think and feel.

Change is not impossible. People who are deathly afraid of heights have learned to ride a glass elevator to the top of a skyscraper. They have learned the risk is negligible and the view is incredible. People with phobias of spiders or airplanes or bridges have been taught how to experience and enjoy normal life without terror. People with phobias can learn to grow out of them.

Relationship dependency is really a phobia of being alone. We have seen many people over our decades of counseling learn to push through their fears. We have been privileged to watch as they embraced the essential value of their own self-worth. On this solid, personal foundation, they have restored and entered into relationships with something precious to give—not acts of subservience or demands of control but the gift of a healthy self who understands, experiences, and gives love.

This information on the brain and relationship dependency was not meant to convince you that you are hopelessly addicted. If you have come away with a fatalistic idea that you cannot change because your brain has been altered, this is your dependency talking. Refuse to listen.

We present this understanding of the brain so you have a context for your behaviors. Understanding the factors—emotional and physical—that contribute to certain behaviors, either within a single relationship or within a relational revolving door, is important. We also want to encourage you that, because you have trained your brain to react in a predetermined way, you can retrain your brain to respond differently. If retraining a brain was impossible, there would be no recovering alcoholics or drug addicts or gamblers or shoppers or overeaters. We know retraining a brain can happen because we have witnessed recovery and change on a regular basis through our work and the work of colleagues across the country.

When we work with someone who is fearful of heights, we help that person understand that climbing stairs or riding in an elevator will not result in injury or death. We help the person understand the flawed nature of their own internal dialogue. We help them realize that the outcomes they tell themselves are inevitable if they climb those stairs or ride in that elevator are not true. Once they recognize how much control they have over their feelings of pleasure and distress, we help them retrain their brain.

In the same way, you can understand that your internal dialogue, which predicts disaster if you are not in a relationship or if you are alone, is not true. You can take control by climbing back into the driver's seat of your life and directing your brain to respond differently, to create a new template for what is pleasurable and what is frightening, inside and outside of a relationship.

Connection Point

We have shown the cyclic pattern that contributes to relationship dependency. We would like you to draw what the cycle of relationship dependency looks like for you. This could be a cycle repeated within a single relationship or a cycle repeated as you move from relationship to relationship.

1. What is your cycle?
2. What starts your cycle?
3. What creates pleasure or relief within that cycle?
4. How is that pleasure or relief destroyed?
5. What do you do to bring that pleasure or relief back?
6. What do you do if you are unable to find relief?

We understand that each person is different, and the factors and triggers contributing to your dependency cycle can be different as well. Personalize your dependency cycle. Become familiar with it. In this way, you'll learn not only to recognize what is propelling you to each step but also to be alert to what could be coming next in your cycle. Avoiding what's coming is easier when you have an idea what it is.

Your brain needs to learn how to respond differently. To do that, you need to experience emotions you have been fearful of in the past. Hopefully, you will begin to understand that experiencing those emotions is necessary so you can choose a different path. And when you are able to claim a win on this path to recovery, your brain will reward you.

8

What Is the Role of Attachment Styles in Relationship Dependency?

A few years ago, I (Dr. Tim) wrote a book with my colleague Dr. Gary Sibcy called *Why You Do the Things You Do: The Secret to Healthy Relationships*. In it, we said that the underlying reason we do the things we do is our relationship style or, to use a word we counselors often use, our attachment style. That book outlined four distinct attachment styles stemming from childhood experiences. We (Dr. Tim and Dr. Gregg) knew we needed to include a chapter on attachment styles because of the connections we've seen between attachment styles and relationship dependency. (For a more comprehensive overview of attachment theory and attachment styles, we encourage you to read *Why You Do the Things You Do: The Secret to Healthy Relationships*.)

Attachment theory highlights the importance of a strong, healthy attachment in childhood. This important attachment comes at the earliest stages of life to a parent or primary caregiver, usually a mother. This first, fundamental attachment, or relationship, sets the stage for all relationships going forward.

When this first, fundamental attachment or relationship is a secure one, the child has a stable platform, a safe base, from which to explore their world. However, if this relationship is not secure, the child must navigate life from an unstable platform, with no safe base to run to when life is tough. When the child attaches to a safe and healthy adult, emotional, physical, and relational stability are provided. But if the child attaches to an unsafe or unhealthy adult, emotional, physical, and relational instability become the norm. This norm may be replicated in future relationships.

A secure attachment also helps a person establish positive values and beliefs about self and others. An insecure attachment can cause a person to establish negative values and beliefs about self and others. Because relationships are connections between self and others, this initial attachment and the core values established, either positive or negative, have long-lasting implications.

Each of us is hardwired by God to operate best within a safe and secure parent/child attachment or relationship. Obviously, outside events happen that can threaten this safety and stability. Parents and caregivers may become ill, leave, or die. Catastrophic events, outside the control of a parent or caregiver, can rock a child's world. Sadly, when the people who should love us have difficulty doing so, safety and stability in childhood are undermined.

When that first and foundational relationship is threatened—when separation on any level from the primary caregiver occurs—children act predictably. The predictable pattern is first protest, then despair, and finally detachment. Just go to any church nursery on a Sunday morning and you'll see a vivid example of the first part of this pattern, protest. Watch what happens when an infant is dropped off for the first time or even the twenty-first time by a parent or caregiver. Does the child squeal with delight? Not usually. Instead, it is more normal for the infant to protest. Their eyes screw up. Their mouth opens in a wail of protest. They squirm when handed over. They reach frantically back for the parent.

Even though the nursery staff is able to care for the child, the child demands to remain attached to the parent. Safety is hardwired into the child as proximity to the parent. Proximity to the parent means security and comfort. Naturally, as the child grows, the safety perimeter, the proximity, expands. The child tolerates Mommy or Daddy going into the next room, out of sight, because the child has learned they will return.

A young child who has not yet learned that Mommy or Daddy returns feels distress upon separation and protests. On a typical Sunday, the child is soon reunited with the parent and security is reestablished. What happens, though, if Mommy or Daddy does not always return? What happens if the child believes Mommy or Daddy may not return?

When protests do not work and the parent leaves anyway, the child moves into the next stage. Feeling abandoned by the parent, the child lapses into despair. A child in the midst of despair may refuse to participate in activities. They may refuse to eat. They may refuse to interact with others.

If the separation is long enough, or the separation pattern is consistent, the child will eventually become detached. This detachment is not marked by detachment from eating or playing or interacting with others, as in the despair stage. It is marked by detachment from the parent. If or when that person enters back into the child's life, the child can appear disinterested or even display signs of hostility toward the parent. The child may reject the reappearance of the parent and respond only to an object, such as a treat or toy, with delight. They have walled themselves off from being hurt through detachment. They have protected themselves from perceived abandonment through detachment.

Being abandoned hurts. At our youngest age, we experience pain when left and protest against it. When abandonment happens, against our best efforts to protest against it, we can lapse into a state of despair, listless and unengaged in a reality that is causing us so much pain. After a time, however, we begin to surface from that despair but determine to remove ourselves from the possibility of being hurt further. We detach from the painful relationship. We detach from people who are unpredictable and do not respond to our needs. Instead, we may attach to things such as food or toys that seem more predictable.

Your attachment experiences are integral to your ability to form and maintain relationships, even your relationship with yourself. What you experienced as a child in your first and foundational relationship established your attachment style. In *Why You Do the Things You Do: The Secret to Healthy Relationships*, four attachment styles are identified. Which attachment style a person has is based on their answers to four simple questions. These four questions are foundational questions, and people answer them based on their childhood experiences with parents and caregivers.

The first two questions have to do with the *self*:

1. Am I worthy of being loved?
2. Am I able to do what I need to do to get the love I need?

The next two questions have to do with *others*:

3. Are other people reliable and trustworthy?
4. Are other people accessible and willing to respond to me when I need them?[1]

Your answers to these questions lead to one of four attachment styles:

1. secure
2. ambivalent
3. avoidant
4. disorganized

■ The Secure Attachment Style

The secure attachment style is the stable platform, the safe base, of relationships. A person has a secure attachment style if they can answer yes to all four of the questions:

1. Yes, I am worthy of being loved.
2. Yes, I am able to do what I need to do to get the love I need.
3. Yes, other people are reliable and trustworthy.
4. Yes, other people are accessible and willing to respond to me when I need them.

Obviously, no parent is perfect, and no child correctly interprets everything that happens to them. The secure attachment style is not based on perfection; it is based on a pattern in which the parent provides the child with confidence in their self-worth by demonstrating love and acceptance. The attachment style is based on the parent instilling in the child an understanding that they are able to get the love they need by demonstrating that love on a regular, consistent basis. The child learns that other people are reliable and trustworthy when the parent exhibits those characteristics, providing structure and security. Finally, the child becomes secure in relationships when the parent is accessible to the child and willingly responds to the child's needs.

How do you know if you have a secure attachment style? People who have this attachment style exhibit specific characteristics and personality traits. Here is a list of statements for those with a secure attachment style.

Statements for the Secure Attachment Style

1. I find it easy to share my feelings with people I'm close to.
2. I like it when my partner wants to share their feelings with me.
3. I am comfortable getting close to others, but I also feel comfortable being alone.
4. I expect my partner to respect who I am.
5. I expect my partner to respond to my needs in a sensitive and appropriate way.
6. Building intimacy in relationships comes relatively easy for me.

7. I let myself feel my emotions, but I'm rarely, if ever, overwhelmed by them.

8. I am able to understand and respond sensitively to my partner's feelings.

9. I do a decent job balancing my need for intimacy with my need for achievement and success.

10. When I get stressed, I feel comfortable seeking comfort from my partner and/or close friends.

The more you are able to agree with each of these statements, the more secure your attachment style. In our experience, many people are able to agree with several of these statements but not all. If you are unable to agree with all of these statements, don't be discouraged. Each of us can work toward a greater fulfillment of the benefits of secure attachment.

Secure Attachment and Intimacy

When a person believes they are worthy to receive and give love and that others are willing and able to do the same, security is possible. With mutual love and security, intimacy and deep emotional connection flourish.

- A person with a secure attachment style is secure in who they are and their worth as a person. Out of this security, they choose a relationship with someone who loves and values them. Within this cocoon of security, they are comfortable with and invite closeness.

- With a foundation of love and acceptance, they are not afraid to share their feelings and dreams. In fact, they are eager to do so because they trust the other person to respond with honesty and support.

- With security, the future is something to be anticipated with enthusiasm, not feared with trepidation. Because of their belief in a positive future, they are willing to commit themselves to others.

- Because they know and like themselves, they are able to balance times of intimacy and closeness with those needed times of introspection and distance. They are not afraid to pull away for a time because they are assured of their reception when they return.

- They are secure in themselves and in the relationship and do not feel a need to "purchase" the relationship through sexual barter. They understand that intimacy and sexuality can be expressed in a variety of ways and are comfortable with participating in nonsexual touch.

Safe, secure, loved, and accepted—these are the hallmarks of secure attachment. Is it any wonder that people search over and over again to obtain it through sometimes flawed methods?

Secure Attachment Emotions

- A person with a secure attachment style is able to experience a full range of emotions because their life is not dominated by the negative emotions of fear, distrust, resentment, and anger. Optimism, hope, and joy can be fully explored within their secure attachment to self and to others.

- They are able to learn and exhibit control over their emotions. They are not completely overwhelmed or undone by strong emotional currents. If happy, they are able to laugh and enjoy the moment. If sad, they are able to grieve and express their loss. While they may swing between the poles of positive and negative because of life circumstances, they do not swing wildly out of control.

- They are able to recognize their ability to self-soothe. While they will accept the reassurance and comfort of others, they are also able to give themselves those gifts as well. Because they love and accept themselves, they are able to use those positive affirmations to give context to their distress and avoid catastrophic thinking.

- Because they are in control of their emotions, they are able to share those feelings with others. They are not fearful of becoming emotional with others because they understand the boundaries of healthy emotions. They do not hold their emotions with others for ransom, requiring certain preconditions before sharing their inner thoughts and emotional responses. They are able to use their emotions to draw people into a relationship with them, instead of using their emotions to force people away.

- Because they are comfortable with who they are and with their own emotions, they are able to experience the feelings of others without fear. They are able to share emotional contexts with others in order for both parties to understand each other better and deepen the relationship.

■ The Ambivalent Attachment Style

A person with an ambivalent attachment style answers the four questions this way:

1. No, I am not worthy of being loved.
2. No, I am not able to do what I need to do to get the love I need unless I demand it.
3. No, other people are not reliable and trustworthy because I am not worthy.
4. Yes, other people can be accessible and respond to me when I need them but only if I force them to through my behavior.

An ambivalent attachment style comes from a childhood in which love and affection are inconsistently given, based on factors the child does not understand. Love and affection, though desperately wanted by the child, are seen as incredibly fragile things that can vanish without warning. Because the child is never sure of receiving love and affection, they have an overriding necessity to secure the insecure.

A child who is unsure of love and lives with the constant fear of abandonment grows up ambivalent toward relationships. They desire something of which they are fundamentally fearful. In ambivalent relationships, there is no safety. Love and acceptance one day do not guarantee love and acceptance the next day, even under identical circumstances. The only constant the child has on which to affix blame for this inconsistency is self. The child concludes that love is withheld because they are not good enough or smart enough, are not trying hard enough, or have not communicated strongly enough. There is no security in the relationship with the parent because that person may leave or withdraw love and affection at any time.

Here are the statements that describe those with an ambivalent attachment style.

Statements for the Ambivalent Attachment Style

1. I really like sharing my feelings with my partner, but they do not seem as open as I am.
2. My feelings can get out of control quickly.
3. I worry about being alone.
4. I worry about being abandoned in close relationships.
5. My partner complains that I am too clingy and emotional.
6. I strongly desire to be very intimate with people.
7. In my closest relationships, the other person doesn't seem as desirous of intimacy and closeness as I am.
8. I worry a great deal about being rejected by others.
9. I tend to value close, intimate relationships over personal achievement and success.
10. When I get stressed, I desperately seek others for support, but no one seems as available as I would like them to be.

A person with an ambivalent attachment style is constantly looking for proof of love and affection. They are distrustful of others and seek to verify the relationship, often with extreme behaviors that can backfire and alienate the other person. Because the relationship seems always in jeopardy, the ambivalent person tends to focus obsessively on the relationship. How is it going? Are there any problems? Did I do everything right? How does the other person feel about me? No amount of reasonable reassurance seems enough, and the person appears needy and clingy while at the same time capable of extreme anger and rage.

Ambivalent Attachment and Intimacy

An ambivalent person does not believe they are worthy of or able to receive love on their own. They believe the only way to achieve love is to manipulate others through behavior. Approval, love, and affection must be coerced or tricked out of others who would not normally extend them because the ambivalent person is convinced of their unworthiness. This manipulative view of others creates havoc in relationships and damages the conditions vital for intimacy.

- A person with an ambivalent attachment style desires closeness and attempts to manipulate circumstances to receive that closeness. Because that closeness is manufactured, they distrust its authenticity. The artificiality of the closeness ends up negating its effects so that even though there is closeness, there never seems to be enough.

- Without a true foundation in self, the ambivalent person seeks solidity in intimacy through merging with another person. If they are able to merge with someone else, then that person should become tied to them. They see those ties as binding them together, while the other person may see those ties as strangulation.

- Convinced of the truth of their unworthiness to be in a relationship, they are preoccupied with abandonment. This preoccupation pollutes the intimate atmosphere by continually interjecting doubt and fear of rejection.

- Fearful of the very intimacy they crave, they both cling to and criticize the other person.

Ambivalent Attachment Emotions

- Because a person with an ambivalent attachment style has experienced some level of accessibility and response, they know people are capable of giving them. However, because that accessibility and response have been inconsistent, they believe they are responsible for that inconsistency. When others treat them well, they are able to experience joy and delight and learn to seek after those rare moments with all the determination of a miner panning for gold.

- The inconsistency experienced in accessibility and response from others, however, creates an ongoing fear of rejection. Without a sense of security, they feel disaster is only a moment away. Because of this, they hold their panic and fear on a short leash, ready to put them in the forefront at a moment's notice. While they desperately want to stay in a positive emotional space, their fear is constantly pushing them toward the negative, resulting in poor emotional control.

- With disaster just a moment away, they find it impossible to self-soothe. They cannot talk themselves away from the edge of disaster because disaster is all they see surrounding them. They live on the edge. Because they are always in a heightened state of alert, they are not able to calm themselves down.

- Emotional highs are experienced like hitting the jackpot. Emotional lows are experienced as catastrophic events. Without a compass to help them navigate passage through a middle ground, they swing wildly from side to side, from dark to light, from ecstasy to disaster.

153

In this pumped-up emotional state, they aren't able to shut down the flood of emotions, either good or bad, and end up flooding themselves and others with their feelings.

- In this oversaturated emotional environment, any additional emotional content from other people sends them over the brink, and they become overwhelmed by others' feelings.

■ The Avoidant Attachment Style

Just as those with an ambivalent attachment style tend to cling voraciously to others, those with an avoidant attachment style tend to cling voraciously to self. Because of the emotional, physical, and/or relational unavailability of a parent, the avoidant person has concluded that they must handle life solo. Here is how an avoidant person answers the four questions:

1. Yes, I am worthy of being loved not for who I am but for what I can do.
2. Yes, I am able to do what I need to do to get the love I need because I give it to myself.
3. No, other people are not reliable and trustworthy, so I need to rely only on myself.
4. No, other people are not accessible and willing to respond to me when I need them, so I need to take care of myself.

An avoidant person, when faced with abandonment in any form, determines never again to be placed in such a position of need. The panic and pain of rejection are protested against by burial of those negative feelings. The anger produced at the pain and rejection can fuel social isolation, emotional detachment, and perfectionism. The avoidant person constructs massive barriers to intimacy as a way to shelter self from additional pain. The avoidant person learns to deal with relationships as tasks, as check-off-the-box exercises, and avoids the deeper emotional context, remaining present in a relationship but distant.

Statements for the Avoidant Attachment Style

1. I don't like sharing my feelings with others.
2. I don't like it when my partner wants to talk about their feelings.
3. I have a hard time understanding how other people feel.
4. When I get stressed, I try to deal with the situation all by myself.
5. My partner often complains that I don't like to talk about how I feel.
6. I don't really need close relationships.
7. I highly value my independence and self-sufficiency.
8. I don't worry about being alone or abandoned.
9. I don't worry about being accepted by others.
10. I tend to value personal achievements and success over close, intimate relationships.

Relying solely on self may appear to be an effective way to get your needs met. Why rely on others if others only let you down? This thinking misses the essence of a relationship—the connection between two people. The reason an avoidant person misses this connection is because the connection was not present in their first and foundational relationship. An ambivalent person knows that the parent will be available part of the time at least. An avoidant person learns that the parent will not be available, period. In order to provide structure and security in such an environment, the avoidant person learns to rely not on relationships but on self. Are these people self-reliant? Yes, to the extreme, and they are also relationship avoidant.

What does a person do who has learned totally to rely on self? What do they do when they mess up? An avoidant person, with no one else to blame, may resort to narcissism (a falsely elevated sense of self), introversion (unaccountable to others), or perfectionism (rigidly accountable to self). The narcissist elevates self at the expense of others, believing self to be superior. To avoid the anxiety of relying on others to provide love and acceptance, the narcissist may seek out and manipulate others for approval. While it may appear that these individuals are not avoidant but actually like to be around people, the opposite is true. The narcissist uses people to build up and fortify self, which is their only relational goal. The narcissist may be engaging, funny, and charismatic, but the only true relationship the person has is with an inflated sense of self.

An avoidant person may also become an introvert, one who crawls into a hole of self-sufficiency. Because the introvert does not trust others, others are to be avoided. The introvert shuns relationships with others and instead substitutes things or activities for connection and pleasure. People, as the avoidant person has learned, are unreliable, so people must be avoided. Things, on the other hand, can be controlled and manipulated and therefore are more secure. Because the introvert rejects relationships, the introvert is unsure of their own emotions, preferring to suppress them in a bland and apathetic attitude.

An avoidant person may also be prone to perfectionism, seeking security and order through performance. If your self-worth becomes tied not to who you are but to what you do, then can you ever really do enough? If your value in life consists of the content of your performance, then any infraction, any mistake, any miscalculation negatively detracts from that value. Perfectionism becomes a way to "prove" your value to those who gave you none.

Narcissism is a way for the avoidant person to say, "I don't need you because I'm better than you." Isolationism is a way for the avoidant person to say, "I don't need you because you don't mean that much to me." Perfectionism is a way for the avoidant person to say, "I don't need you because I can do it all myself."

Avoidant Attachment and Intimacy

An avoidant person does not see value in other people and therefore sees no value in intimacy. Intimacy is too close, too revealing, too dangerous. Intimacy, if tolerated at all, is seen as a task to be performed in order to achieve a prespecified objective. For the avoidant person, intimacy becomes not so much what you do for others but what you do for yourself.

- A person with an avoidant attachment style views physical intimacy as a means to an end but does not even contemplate opening themselves up to emotional intimacy. Closeness is extremely uncomfortable and is only minimally tolerated.

- They consider their physical proximity to another person the only acceptable intimacy and will tenaciously hold on to their own feelings and dreams.
- Though they may go through the motions of physical intimacy, they hold their inner self in reserve, refusing to risk any level of transparency and commitment. Commitment, seen as capitulation and personal surrender, becomes extremely uncomfortable.
- When their core barriers are threatened, either by the actions and emotions of others or by their own actions and emotions, they withdraw behind those barriers, distancing themselves from the other person and the emotions that person may have stirred.

Avoidant Attachment Emotions

- An avoidant person avoids emotions, so they do not display the emotional content a reasonable person would expect. Their demeanor is flat or blunted. They may appear disconnected and apathetic toward others.
- Reining in their emotions is like taking a tiger by the tail; such an effort requires constant vigilance. Their focus, then, becomes controlling their emotions so as not to display weakness or give too much of themselves away.
- When controlling and focusing fail and emotions threaten to overwhelm, the avoidant person uses things to self-soothe. They have found that things are more secure than people and will turn to those sure things in isolation.
- Because emotions are unstable and dangerous, they attempt to keep emotions deeply buried. The deeper the

pit, the less likely those emotions are to surface and cause trouble. In order to keep their emotions buried as deep as possible, they cover them with layers and layers of rituals and obligations that must be performed perfectly.

- Because they shy away from emotions and have buried them so deep, they are no longer able to share feelings and are fearful of unearthing and articulating them to self or others.

The Disorganized Attachment Style

The disorganized attachment style can best be described as none of the above. A disorganized person is a hodgepodge of responses without a consistent pattern. If there is a pattern, it is that there is no pattern. The disorganized person has come to view relationships, often because of the presence of abuse, as a source of both comfort and fear. As a result, they may vacillate between a secure response one minute and an avoidant response the next. A disorganized person is in conflict and answers the four questions this way:

1. No, I am not worthy of being loved.
2. No, I am not able to do what I need to do to get the love I need.
3. No, other people are not reliable and trustworthy.
4. No, other people are not accessible and willing to respond to me when I need them.

Because there is no surety anywhere, a disorganized person will use whatever strategy they think might work at any given time, bouncing from one to another, trying anything to gain relational ground.

Statements for the Disorganized Attachment Style

1. My feelings are very confusing to me, so I try not to feel them.
2. My feelings are very intense and overwhelming.
3. I feel torn between wanting to be close to others and wanting to pull away.
4. My partner complains that sometimes I'm really needy and clingy and other times I'm distant and aloof.
5. I have a difficult time letting others get close to me, but once I let them in, I worry about being abandoned or rejected.
6. I feel very vulnerable in close relationships.
7. Sometimes I feel very disconnected from myself and my feelings.
8. I can't decide whether or not I want to be in close relationships.
9. Other people can really hurt me if I let them get too close.
10. Close relationships are difficult to come by because people tend to be unpredictable in their actions and behaviors.

A disorganized person lives a life of crisis and chaos. A moment of calm is distrusted and may be subconsciously sabotaged in order for them to return to the chaotic, to the known and the "normal." When chaos is normal, the emotional turmoil that accompanies chaos and trauma can also become normal.

Constantly inundated by an avalanche of intense emotions, the disorganized person learns to dissociate from them, essentially detaching from their emotions. As the disorganized person detaches from their emotions, they become less able to recognize, manage, or control those emotions. The more they detach from the emotional self, the less they are able to learn from experiences. The less they are able to learn from experiences, the more vulnerable they become to repeating past mistakes and miscalculations. The more they repeat past mistakes and miscalculations, the more this cycle is intensified and the less grasp on self the disorganized person is able to maintain. In *Why You Do the Things You Do: The Secret to Healthy Relationships*, the disorganized attachment style is also called the shattered self.

Disorganized Attachment and Intimacy

To a disorganized person, no one is trustworthy. Everyone is suspect, and emotions are only valuable when they are used to gain what they want. A disorganized person lives behind a series of masks used to camouflage the shattered self.

- Without a sense of their own identity, they seek out the closeness of others as a substitute. However, because they distrust the other person and themselves, they fear closeness and find ways to avoid it.
- Conflicted about who they are, they vacillate between desperately wanting to find relief through merging with another person and needing to create distance out of fear.
- Living within an atmosphere of negativity about self and others, they become convinced of their own worthlessness and the inability or unwillingness of others

161

to rescue them from it. Everyone is suspect, and they remain rooted in overwhelming fear of abandonment.

- Rather than suffer the pain of rejection and abandonment, they find ways to sabotage closeness, creating artificial proof of the only sure thing in this world—that no one can be trusted.

- Seeking after some measure of surety in the world, they seek out people who will "prove" their basic, negative assumptions. Instead of taking a risk on people who might do the unexpected and love them, they are attracted, instead, to the sure, to the known, to people who will victimize them.

Disorganized Attachment Emotions

- A person with a disorganized attachment style has experience with the full range of emotions and will use whatever one fits the best in order to try to get their needs met. While they know the positive emotions, they most commonly live with the negative emotions.

- Because they put on their emotions like outerwear, they are quick to switch from emotion to emotion, exhibiting poor control and finding it difficult to stay in one emotional context.

- The instability they bring to their emotions results in an inability to create a lasting environment for the positive. The negative is so quick to appear, meaning they are unable to self-soothe.

- Aware that other people are not so quick to switch from one emotional state to another without an apparent or appropriate reason, they know emotions are an avenue for others to uncover the truth. True emotions, then, become dangers and cannot be shared with others.

- Juggling so many potential emotional responses to life in order to control circumstances is hard work. There are simply too many of their own emotional balls to keep in the air. The thought of adding in the emotions of others is overwhelming.
- When overwhelmed with the stress and strain of emotional juggling, they begin to detach themselves from the emotional onslaught, dissociating from themselves in order to provide distance from the pain.

Connection Point

If you haven't done so yet, answer the four basic questions:

1. Am I worthy of being loved?
2. Am I able to do what I need to do to get the love I need?
3. Are other people reliable and trustworthy?
4. Are other people accessible and willing to respond to me when I need them?

Have those always been your answers? What would you have said as a child? As a teenager? As a young adult? If an answer has changed, can you identify when the shift occurred and why? What happened to cause you to change that belief about yourself or others?

Look at the statements and points for each attachment style and circle the ones that are true for you. Look at them again and put a star next to the ones you want to be true for you.

You've been asked to get to know yourself better, to put a style to the way you experience yourself and others. Now that you've identified an attachment style, is that attachment style enough for you? Or do you see a need to find a way to feel and act differently? Are you ready to find a way to love yourself and others better? What you've discovered about attachment styles is your present based in your past. What you've discovered doesn't need to be your future.

9

How Spiritual Dependency Overcomes Relationship Dependency

As we have said, the core of relationship dependency is a belief that you, by yourself, are not enough. We hope you have seen how the strategy of using others—of using relationships—to provide wholeness does not work. People change; people leave; people refuse; people reject. While this strategy of using others may help you momentarily fill the void of self, this strategy is not a lasting solution. The strategy of using others doesn't save you; it damages you and your relationships.

We were not meant to be alone, as the apostle Paul, in Ephesians 2:12, says. The bleakness of separation is not good, as Genesis 2:18 echoes. Yes, we were meant for relationships, but we were meant for relationships built on love. Those who are relationship dependent enter into and attempt to maintain relationships out of fear. As Christians, we believe fear-based relationships, with self and others, are not the relationships God intended. Dependent people may be well-intentioned and seek love within relationships, but fear has a way of overwhelming those best intentions.

When fear is your motivation for a relationship, your actions and attitudes threaten to take the shape of desperation, panic, frustration, and resentment. Your relationships can center on forestalling those fears. When you are in a survival mode in a relationship, you may desperately try to hold your fears at bay. When desperation kicks in, your focus on the relationship becomes self-centered; the other person can become just a means to an end—the end of fear, the end of loneliness, the end of abandonment.

How damaging is it to live in a relationship with profound insecurity? When each day is a potential disaster, when every person is suspect, when all actions are flawed and each thought is catastrophic, there can be no peace, no security. If you live with overwhelming fear, you may decide that the only way to attain a shadow of peace and security is through rigid control. You may try to control the pain by saying yes even when you mean no. You may try to control the pain by being perfect even when you're not. You may try to control the pain by tying yourself to needy people. Through all of this, you may try to hide your true fears by wearing an everything-is-fine mask.

Dependency and God

There is one relationship impervious to masks. You may fool some of the people all of the time or all of the people some of the time, but you cannot fool God. The damage of dependency infects all relationships, including your relationship with God. Many dependent people believe in God, but they fear God as the ultimate authority figure. In their minds, God is the über-parent who sees and punishes every fault, who eternally withholds love, acceptance, and approval. Do you believe you will never measure up, never do enough, to receive God's love? As much as you want God's approval, are you convinced you will never receive it?

Many of the dependent people of faith we've helped over the years lived with a partial understanding of God. They understood God as all-powerful and holy but failed to recognize God's love and grace. They readily latched on to spiritual concepts of unworthiness while missing the gift of God's forgiveness. As Christians, we believe we can never do enough to merit God's love. We cannot "purchase" salvation; that is why we need a Savior.

If you are a dependent person of faith, you may have difficulty accepting God's grace. The definition of grace is unmerited favor. Underlying dependency is a belief that you do not deserve such unmerited favor. You may distrust your ability to be perfect, and you may distrust God's willingness to love, accept, approve of, and forgive you. You may believe in God but discount and distrust his grace, mercy, and forgiveness, fundamental elements of God's nature.

When working with people of faith who struggle with dependency issues, we have found tremendous benefit in addressing these deep-seated spiritual fears and misconceptions. Is it true that we are unworthy of God's love? Yes, but that is only part of the truth. We are unworthy of God's love, yet Scripture also clearly tells us that we are, nonetheless, loved by God. One of the most-quoted verses in the New Testament is John 3:16: "For God so loved the world that he gave his one and only Son, that whoever believes in him shall not perish but have eternal life."

We are unworthy of God's love, yet he loves us anyway. How can that be? God loves each one of us not because of who we are but because of who he is. God is the epitome of love. Dependent people often have great difficulty believing that something that good can be true. Even though they want to believe, they say they've been burned too many times. Do you feel that way? Do you desperately want to believe God loves and accepts you but are terrified he can't or won't? Are you afraid that, at the last minute, God will do what so many others have done and pull the rug of approval out from under you? If you feel this way, trust is a huge spiritual issue. The dependent people we've worked with have painstakingly learned how to experience what we call the free fall of faith, learning to trust that God's grace is able to catch their fall.

Trusting in God may be a challenge for you if you're more comfortable trusting in your own spiritual efforts. You may have decided that if you do the "right" things, then God will be obligated to approve of you. If you fulfill your religious obligations (i.e., go to church, help the needy, not curse, pray, read the Bible, give money, visit the sick, etc.), then God must keep his end of the bargain (i.e., allow nothing bad to happen to you or those you love). You may have reduced the gift of salvation to a mere contract with God. God has become your spiritual business partner.

Life, however (or God for that matter), simply does not work this way. Bad things happen, no matter how many religious obligations you fulfill. God, who is neither a divine genie nor a spiritual Santa, does not reside in heaven filling orders. When life doesn't happen according to the "contract," you may become disillusioned with God or even angry with God. Disillusionment with God erodes your faith even further.

◼ Taking Spiritual Matters into Your Own Hands

What do people do when it seems as though God is not acting according to their expectations? When people think God is not acting according to the "contract," they often take spiritual matters into their own hands. If God is not acting the way he's supposed to, then it's time to trade him in for a different model, even if they have to make that different model themselves. This trading in God for something else has a religious name—idolatry.

Idolatry is not only taking something bad and trying to make it something good. Idolatry is also taking a good thing and turning it into an ultimate thing. Turning away from God and to a relationship as a way to save yourself is spiritually dangerous. We have found this type of idolatry present in dependent relationships. We have witnessed the sense of panic dependent people can feel at even the thought of change to a relationship.

An idolater takes something unable to save them, like a piece of wood or stone, and fashions it into the essence of personal salvation. A dependent person takes something unable to save them, like a human relationship, and fashions it into the essence of personal salvation. An idolater etches into the stone or wood what they desperately want. A dependent person etches into the other person what they desperately want. Neither finds what they're looking for because both are looking in the wrong place.

There is nothing inherently wrong in wanting loving, caring relationships—as long as the pursuit doesn't consume you. There is nothing inherently wrong in wanting loving, caring relationships—as long as those relationships don't become a substitute for God.

If you struggle with dependency, looking to others to provide approval, validation, assurance, relief, and significance can become a painful, addictive cycle. But it need not be. All of these—validation, assurance, relief, significance, and so much more—are gifts from God.

When other people are expected to provide these gifts, those people have a way of coming up short. When those people come up short, dependent people believe they must put up with irresponsible and even abusive behaviors out of love. Christians may even believe they must overlook those irresponsible or abusive behaviors, thinking doing so is the right spiritual thing to do.

There are reasons why you might enter into or continue in a dependent relationship. You may feel safest in a clearly defined role. For example, you may continue in a dependent relationship because you feel safe in the role of provider or even in the role of victim. Victims, after all, have a right to demand justice, attention, and guarantees. These can be the very things you want and need from others. The suffering you endure in the relationship may even give you a sense of self-righteousness or superiority. This victim perspective may feel right to you, may give you a sense of power and control. But this victim perspective blocks healing, growth, forgiveness, and an opportunity for genuine reconciliation in relationships.

Giving up a victim identity can appear risky. You may desire to continue in the victim role, often misunderstanding Scripture to maintain the status quo. Some dependent Christians have turned the other cheek so often they're like oscillating fans—and the person who is using and abusing them feels completely justified and powerful, deepening the enmeshment of the relationship.

Some dependent Christians mistakenly equate the suffering of dependency with religious suffering or suffering for Christ. Staying in the relationship, even amid profound suffering, becomes a religious imperative. When this happens, the victim identity becomes a martyr identity. Such people often have difficulty detaching from this identification as a martyr. This martyr complex can be especially strong in close family relationships, such as between spouses or a parent and child.

God is especially particular about relationships. As Christians, we believe there is only one God, and his name is Jealous (Exod. 34:14). There is only one Savior, and his name is Jesus (Titus 3:6). There are no substitutes; there is no other name under heaven (Acts 4:12) for true salvation. When we attempt to substitute anything else in our lives—and there are many options today—we have fallen into the trap of present-day idolatry.

Getting rid of the idols in our lives is never easy. However, putting aside the false things we trust in and turning that trust over to God are acts of sincere faith. Both of us have seen the transforming power of faith in the lives of dependent people, so we know this transformation is possible. We deeply believe the transformation that needs to take place is for you to move from being relationally dependent to being spiritually dependent.

■ Replacing Relationship Dependency with Spiritual Dependency

Spiritual dependency can replace relationship dependency when the truth of God is followed not partway but all the way to the end. Yes, we are unworthy, but we have never been unlovable because God has loved us from the very beginning. How can we be sure of that love? God demonstrated that love by giving us Jesus.

In chapter 4, you read about the fears of dependency. The voice of dependency speaks half and false truths born out of those fears. We encourage you, instead of listening to the fearful voice of dependency, to begin to listen to the voice of love from God. When you listen to God's voice, you can move from unhealthy relationship dependency to God's truth of spiritual dependency. Following are spiritual concepts based on our Christian beliefs that we have used to counter the fearful voice of dependency.

Fear says do everything you can to avoid exposure; love says you are known and accepted just as you are.

With God, there is nowhere to hide. God is everywhere and sees everything. Psalm 139 is a poetic love song about a loving God who knit you together in your mother's womb. Are you now and have you always been exposed before God? Of course! He knows everything about you and loves you still. Exposure to God is not something to be feared. You never have to be fearful that something you do or say will make God love you less.

Fear says you have no identity; love says your identity is a child of God.

We are often tempted to base our identity on family or jobs or accomplishments, even transitory things such as physical attractiveness. But deep down, these things are not who we are. Deep down, we know these are not enough to build a real identity. In this fear that we are really empty—as an emperor with no clothes—we may try to fill up the emptiness with other things, such as relationships. When dependency tries to tell you that you're nothing on your own, that is a lie! You are someone, whether you are in a relationship or not.

Your identity will never come from transitory, earthly things because your true nature is not earthly but eternal. We are spiritual beings in earthly bodies. There will come a time when family will not matter, nor will work or accomplishments, and there will certainly come a time when how you look won't matter. Fear seeks to keep you trapped in the earthly. The truth of your identity is found in the eternal. One of the most liberating realizations a dependent person can come to is that they are loved by God, and not only loved but claimed by God as his child.

Fear says you are destined to be abandoned; love says, "Never will I leave you" (Heb. 13:5).

You may have a powerful fear of being abandoned. Abandonment means being left to your own devices, and you're terrified those devices are not enough to protect you. Abandonment equals catastrophe. Fear says you will be abandoned; love says you never are. From the Old Testament to the New Testament, from Deuteronomy to Hebrews, God promises his constant presence.

People may leave, and earthly abandonment is a condition too often suffered in this world. But God does not abandon those he loves, and he loves you. Love does not abandon its own. Think back to the famous passage on love in 1 Corinthians 13, to the four "always" and the one "never" written about love: Love "always protects, always trusts, always hopes, always perseveres. Love never fails" (vv. 7–8). Always, always, always, always, never. These are not the words of abandonment; these are the words of permanence.

Fear says you will be rejected; love says you are accepted by God.

Love is given by God to each of us because of who he is, not because of who we are, not because of what we've done. When you look in the mirror, you may see a flawed, unlovable human being. That's not what God sees; God sees his beloved child.

If you intentionally pull away from God and make yourself a "victim" of his condemnation and wrath, you are falling into dependency's trap. This trap says you must reject God first to avoid his inevitable rejection. If you don't really trust in God's love, then you reject who God is. If you reject who God is, then you reject the reassurance of what you desperately need—and already have: God's love.

Fear says you are worthless; love says you are priceless.

One of the debilitating fears of dependency is the fear that you have no value. You may try to gain a sense of significance through those you're with, but true value comes in being a child of God.

When you doubt yourself, remember, "But God chose the foolish things of the world to shame the wise; God chose the weak things of the world to shame the strong" (1 Cor.

1:27). Remember also the words of Jesus from the Sermon on the Mount. He called the poor in spirit, the meek and the mourner, the hungry, the thirsty, and the persecuted blessed (Matt. 5:1–11). God's view of what is blessed, of what is beautiful, of who is significant is at odds with the view of the world. Stop listening to the voice of dependency and fear; start listening to the voice of God. You are blessed; you are beautiful; you are significant.

Fear says security can be lost in the blink of an eye; love says security is found in God.

Security can be intangible, but security is something we often want to hold on to physically. When life becomes a roller coaster, we want a grab bar. God can seem like an intangible, invisible grab bar. We may know his promises, but when we're careening through a crisis, other things seem more secure. We are tempted to turn to work, to food, to play, to technology, to other people to provide stability.

Fear has a way of telling us that a bird in the hand is worth two in the bush. In a crisis, God's promises of love and security can seem less in the hand and more like bush territory. Better to rely on the person or the drink or the drug or the task or the food that we can see, touch, taste, and hold. Trusting in God's security is an act of faith. Faith, as Hebrews 11:1 says, "is confidence in what we hope for and assurance about what we do not see."

The birds in the hand of this world may seem more secure, but God is the true Rock. In Scripture, especially in the Psalms, God is described in terms such as rock (Ps. 18:2), refuge (Ps. 62:8), fortress (Ps. 46:7), shield (Ps. 84:11), and stronghold (Ps. 18:2). These are terms of strength, stability, and protection whose duration is not in the moment but forever.

Fear says if people leave, you are hopelessly adrift; love says you have an anchor.

If you struggle with dependency, then you may gain your sense of identity and worth through other people. When, as invariably happens, those people disengage or die, your connection to value, worth, and identity can be abruptly severed. Tying your value and worth to others is about as secure as a tent peg in a tornado.

Within the vicious cycle of relationship dependency, there is always the fear that the tent peg is going to break loose and the connection to that person be lost. This is why you may spend a great deal of time testing the strength of the tent peg, of the relationship. You may spend time and energy watching for signs of stormy weather in gestures, comments, and actions as you continually test thoughts and feelings.

God has already created an indelible and unbreakable connection between himself and you. Hebrews 6:19 calls this hope "an anchor for the soul, firm and secure." Your connection to other things you value can be lost in the blink of an eye, in weather that seems both fair and foul. But God's connection to you is solid, anchored in his love for you.

Fear says never lose control; love says God is in control.

Fear says you must never lose control, but that fear is a false fear. The loss of control is a false fear because there are so many things you don't have control over. How can you lose something you never had? You want to believe you have full control over your life. Then something bad happens.

When something bad happens, you may try many ways to regain control. When those attempts fail, you may cry out to God to save you. When you cry out to God to save you, you acknowledge the truth that God is really in control.

Secure Spiritual Attachment

Over and over again, the Bible calls God sovereign, which means he has unlimited power and authority. To move from relationship dependency to spiritual dependency, you must acknowledge who or what has true power or authority over you. When you come to believe in and trust in God's love for you, you are able to form a secure spiritual attachment. This secure spiritual attachment is possible no matter what sort of attachment you've had in your earthly relationships.

Do you remember the attachment questions from chapter 8? Let's look at them from a spiritual attachment.

1. *Am I worthy of being loved?* You are loved because God loves you. You no longer need to be "worthy" in order to be loved. This first fundamental question becomes simply, Am I loved by God? And the answer is a resounding yes!

2. *Am I able to do what I need to do to get the love I need?* Since you are loved by God, you already have the love you need. No longer must you perform or manipulate or coerce or barter for the love you need. The question becomes, Has God already done everything needed to love me? And the resounding answer is yes!

3. *Are other people reliable and trustworthy?* From an earthly perspective, the answer is often no. From a

spiritual perspective, this question becomes, Is God reliable and trustworthy? The answer always and forever is yes!

4. *Are other people accessible and willing to respond to me when I need them?* From a spiritual perspective, this becomes, Is God accessible and willing to respond to me when I need him? Again, the answer is yes!

Each of these questions, from a spiritual perspective, is answered by God with a resounding yes! God, then, can become the basis for secure attachment. His love can help you create a secure attachment to who you are, to others, and to him.

God has already done everything he needs to love you. Trusting and living in that love, however, require effort on your part. The amount of effort needed to believe in the good news of God and to begin to create a secure attachment based on him will depend on what attachment style you're starting with. Those who tend toward a more secure attachment style will, generally, have an easier time transferring those yeses they ascribe to self and others over to God. Our experience, however, has been that even those who have secure attachments may still struggle with certain aspects of God's nature and promises.

Struggling with understanding and trusting the truth of God, his nature, and his promises is vital, important work. The lies of dependency tell you that you must be perfect in your understanding of God before you can have a relationship with him. This is ridiculous. The only perfection required for a relationship with God is his perfect love, not our perfect understanding!

Knowing God is a process because, though God does not change, we do. As we change and grow and experience life, we have the opportunity for greater spiritual depth and understanding. The spiritual people we were in our twenties are very different from the spiritual people we are now, decades later. Were we any less loved by God in our twenties than we are now? Of course not! We have been, are, and will be loved as we move through our lives and as our understanding of God changes and grows.

This process of growth and change is called transformation (see Rom. 12:2). Transformation is a gift of God for all of us, no matter where we start on our journey of understanding and trusting him. As we come to know God better, we also come to know ourselves better. This increasing knowledge of self can present a unique challenge for those who struggle with dependency issues. The challenge is that the more we learn about God, the more we come to realize we're more flawed than we ever imagined. If you are a dependent person in recovery who is learning more about God, the challenge is not to park on "more flawed." Instead, you need to continue on, integrating that knowledge with an understanding of and a belief in God's assurance that, while you are more flawed than you ever imagined, you are also more loved than you ever dared hope. Understanding both grants you godly humility but also strength, gratitude, and joy.

▦ Connection Point

We believe faith in God comes down to how you answer the fundamental attachment questions. So in this final exercise, we'd like you to look over the four answers given by the ambivalent, avoidant, and disorganized attachment styles and then consider how those answers may impact a person's relationship with God. Then we will remind you of how we interpreted the secure attachment style from a spiritual viewpoint and ask you to comment on what your life would be like if you fully embraced that perspective.

Here are the answers of the ambivalent attachment style. Write down how you think each answer would impact a person's relationship with God.

1. No, I am not worthy of being loved.
2. No, I am not able to do what I need to do to get the love I need unless I demand it.
3. No, other people are not reliable and trustworthy because I am not worthy.
4. Yes, other people can be accessible and respond to me when I need them but only if I force them to through my behavior.

Here are the answers of the avoidant attachment style. Write down how you think each answer would impact a person's relationship with God.

1. Yes, I am worthy of being loved not for who I am but for what I can do.
2. Yes, I am able to do what I need to do to get the love I need because I give it to myself.
3. No, other people are not reliable and trustworthy, so I need to rely only on myself.
4. No, other people are not accessible and willing to respond to me when I need them, so I need to take care of myself.

Here are the answers of the disorganized attachment style. Write down how you think each answer would impact a person's relationship with God.

1. No, I am not worthy of being loved.
2. No, I am not able to do what I need to do to get the love I need.
3. No, other people are not reliable and trustworthy.
4. No, other people are not accessible and willing to respond to me when I need them.

We do not believe that any of these three styles is the attachment God has with you or wants you to have with him. God's desire is for you to enjoy a secure attachment. If you had such a secure attachment with God, how would each of the following answers impact your life and the lives of those you love?

1. God has said I am loved, and his love is a gift, not anything I can earn.
2. God has already done everything required to give me the love I need.
3. God is reliable and trustworthy, always and forever.
4. God is accessible and willing to respond to me when I need him, always and forever.

As you grow in your knowledge and understanding of and trust in God, we believe you will come closer to that secure attachment with God. This secure attachment is his good, pleasing, and perfect will for you. We are witnesses to the transforming power of God to change people for good. Our prayer is that you will be able to honestly, fervently, and continually pray the prayer below as you journey closer and closer to him.

Dear Lord, Father of relationships, I look to you for grace and truth in all my relationships. Help me to discover the joy you purposed for my relationships. Help me to learn to love myself because you love me. Help me to be wise in my relationships, and guard my relationship with you.

10

How Do You Start Relationship Recovery?

The way to start relationship recovery is to take a step of faith. The late Corrie ten Boom is credited with saying, "Faith is like radar that sees through the fog."[1] Living a life enmeshed in the throes of dependency can be like living in a relational fog. The fears and behaviors of dependency obscure the truth about all of your relationships—with self, others, and God. We challenge you to use faith as radar to help you see through your relational fog. You'll need every ounce of faith you have, because for many of you, the fog of dependency has been forming for years.

The quotation from Corrie ten Boom is especially appropriate for the journey of recovery because, you'll note, she does not say that faith removes the fog. Rather, she says that faith acts like radar that sees through the fog. Entrenched patterns of thought, and the actions those thoughts compel, will not dissipate overnight. Recovery is a journey whose destination, but not path, is fog-free. As you make the journey to your fog-free destination, you will still struggle with fog. However, our hope for you is that you are now more aware the fog exists, more aware of where much of the fog comes from, and have reached the realization that, with faith, you can find your way through.

You've been given opportunities to reflect and write down your thoughts, impressions, revelations, and concerns in the Connection Point sections at the end of each chapter. We want you to use this chapter as a Connection Point for the entire book. Hopefully, you've worked through each chapter. Hopefully, you've come to recognize some personal patterns of dependency and how these patterns can negatively affect your relationships. The fog of dependency may not have lifted yet, but hopefully you're aware that the fog exists—a fog that obscures your view of what positive relationships can be.

Even if you have diligently completed the assignment at the end of each chapter, we encourage you to use the following set of questions as a way to bookmark where you are in your journey up to this point. Where you are now can help you pinpoint where you want to be and the direction you need to take to get there.

The truthful, open, and transparent answers you give can also serve as a road map for others you may be working with on your relationship dependency issues, whether a friend, a pastor, or a therapist. You may be someone who has thought about but has not written down answers in each of the previous Connection Point sections. If so, we encourage you to take the time, the energy, and the courage to complete the following questions.

These questions come from a workshop we did at a recent American Association of Christian Counselors conference, where we made a joint presentation on relationship dependency. We encourage you to take as much time as you need to truthfully answer these questions. Use every bit of information and insight you've gained. As much as you are able, be fearless in acknowledging your life and relationships. Some of these questions you will have answered before, but we want you to answer them again now. Your answers may be the same, but they may also have changed as your understanding has changed.

Remember, this is not a pass-or-fail test. Avoid attempting the black-and-white thinking of absolutes. The only right answer here is a truthful answer.

1. What are your most significant past relationships?
2. What are your most significant relationships now?
3. Do you find yourself focusing your attention and effort on solving other people's problems?
4. Do you routinely put the needs of others above your own?
5. Do you often take responsibility for meeting the needs of others? If so, whose needs?
6. If something goes wrong in your life, do you feel personally responsible?
7. Do you try hard to fulfill the expectations other people have of you?
8. Do you feel like a failure if you aren't able to meet those expectations?
9. Do you consider yourself a person who can recognize and respond to the needs of others?

10. What are your top five needs right now?

11. How often do you voice your own opinions and feelings?

12. If someone expresses an opinion that differs from yours, how do you react?

13. How important is it that other people share what you think and feel?

14. Do you feel uncomfortable expressing an opinion that is different from that of others?

15. What do you do if your opinion differs from that of others?

16. Do you find yourself wearing what you do to please someone else?

17. How important is meeting the expectations of others?

18. Are you the type of person who knows and understands how other people are feeling?

19. Would you say you're devoted to another person? If so, who would that be?

20. How do you feel when you're alone?

21. Do you ever remember a time in your life when you felt abandoned?

22. When other people approve of you, how does that make you feel?

23. How do you feel if other people don't approve of you?

24. Do you feel you have a gift to really love other people?

25. Do you feel your love is strong enough to help other people change?

26. Do you ever dream about what life will be like when the other person changes?

27. What characteristics do you look for in a relationship?

28. As you enter into a new relationship, how much time do you spend thinking about that new relationship?

29. How do you feel about yourself when you are in a relationship? About life in general?

30. In past relationships, how long did it usually take for the honeymoon phase to wear off?

31. When you suspect a relationship may be ending, what do you do to keep it going?

32. When a relationship has ended, what have you been willing to do to rekindle it?

33. How do you feel when a relationship ends?

34. How long does it take for you to enter into another relationship?

35. People have all kinds of fears in life. On a scale of 1 to 10, with 1 being no fear and 10 being absolutely terrified, how would you rate each of the fears below for yourself?
    - fear of loss of control
    - fear of being alone
    - fear of feeling empty
    - fear of being abandoned
    - fear of being rejected
    - fear of being considered insignificant
    - fear of insecurity
    - fear of losing connection to others
    - fear that I am not enough on my own

We ended with the question about fear because understanding your fears is not an end but a step along the way.

Taking a step of faith can replace fear with the knowledge of the love of God. Both of us have the following prayer for you along your journey, the very same prayer the apostle Paul had for the Ephesians:

And [we] pray that you, being rooted and established in love, may have power, together with all the Lord's holy people, to grasp how wide and long and high and deep is the love of Christ, and to know this love that surpasses knowledge—that you may be filled to the measure of all the fullness of God. (3:17–19)

11

Twelve Weeks to Wellness

During the next twelve weeks, we encourage you to make a daily, intentional effort toward fog removal through faith. God's desire is for you to draw near to him, to trust him, and to deepen your relationship with him. We invite you to come to know God and truly begin to know how much he loves you. We believe that when you do, the fears you've been living with and accommodating for years will be revealed for the lies they are. No more cycling from relationship to relationship, no more clinging desperately out of fear to relationships unable to satisfy. You may have anchored your heart, mind, soul, and strength to imperfect patterns of relationship dependency. Now is the time to become independent so you can become truly dependent on God.

Starting wherever you are in the week, right now begin to integrate new patterns into your life, patterns not of relationship dependency but of spiritual dependence. The more you

189

practice the following patterns, the more finely tuned your faith radar will be as you cut through the fog of relationship dependency. Over the next twelve weeks, we ask you to incorporate the following:

- A weekly prayer to learn and hopefully memorize as it sinks deep into your heart, mind, and soul. We find tremendous value in repetition. Repetition allows for the meaning of the words to anchor deep. After all, relationship dependency has been murmuring the same false messages to you over and over again. Now is the time for you to listen to a different message. Now is the time for you to answer back in a different voice. Don't run away from or disparage repetition in prayer. Spiritual truths are like beautiful flowers. At each recitation, these flowers can change and show different aspects of their character, and, like flowers, they may require time to fully unfold. Allow each week's prayer to unfold for you as you meditate on it daily.

- A weekly Scripture passage to help illustrate the love, grace, and mercy of God. We encourage you, instead of merely reading over the words, to meditate on them, looking at them from every facet you can. Memorize them, as you are able, and tuck their truths deep within your heart. (The verses are from the New International Version, but we encourage those of you who are able to look up each verse in multiple versions. Different translations can help enhance understanding.)

- A weekly statement of affirmation, stressing your commitment to growing and changing in this area of dependency. Each statement is based on one of the four attachment questions, affirming God's resounding and loving chorus of yes!

- A "radar of faith" to help you begin to recognize the ways the fog of dependency has obscured your vision of self, others, and God within relationships. Each week, you'll have an opportunity to examine your relationships to detect and deflect unhealthy patterns.

- A weekly action step because faith, as the apostle James says, is not a matter of merely hearing but of doing. Each week, we will encourage you to act in recovery from relationship dependency. You can either use our weekly suggestion or create one of your own, as long as you do it!

- A weekly gratitude list so you can begin to shift focus from the negative to the positive. The fearful, desperate voice of dependency dwells within the fog, alternately whispering or shouting its dreadful negativity. Each week, we'll ask you to pay attention to the truth of God's Spirit and list the positive things you learn about yourself, others, and God. We'll start with three positives for each. Write down at least one example for each category; if you can write down more, great! Remember not to shortchange yourself. God's Spirit has the power to change you from within, so be alert to those changes.

This final encouragement to dwell on the positive is completely biblical. Philippians 4:8 says, "Finally, brothers and sisters, whatever is true, whatever is noble, whatever is right, whatever is pure, whatever is lovely, whatever is admirable— if anything is excellent or praiseworthy—think about such things." Over the next twelve weeks, we ask you to step out in faith and trust the One who is true, noble, right, pure, lovely, admirable, excellent, and praiseworthy. Begin to accept that the One who is all of those things deeply, truly loves you.

Week 1

Prayer

Dear Lord, Father of relationships, I look to you for grace and truth in all my relationships. Help me to discover the joy you purposed for my relationships. Help me to learn to love myself because you love me. Help me to be wise in my relationships, and guard my relationship with you.

Word of Truth

For God so loved the world that he gave his one and only Son, that whoever believes in him shall not perish but have eternal life. (John 3:16)

Affirmation: I am loved by God.

Radar: This week I am seeing the following patterns in my relationships that I need to change to recover from dependency:

Action Step: This week I will allow myself to say, "No, thank you" to a request made of me that I do not want to do.

- The nature of the request:
- The person who made the request:
- How I felt about saying, "No, thank you" to this request:

Gratitude List

The positive things I am learning this week about myself:

1.

2.

3.

The positive things I am learning this week about others:

1.

2.

3.

The positive things I am learning this week about God:

1.

2.

3.

Week 2

Prayer

Holy Father, help me to accept that you are my Father and that you look at me with love. Help me to understand that you see me as your beloved child and that I don't need to be perfect to earn your love. Help me this week to learn to trust in and rest in your love.

Word of Truth

For I am convinced that neither death nor life, neither angels nor demons, neither the present nor the future, nor any powers, neither height nor depth, nor anything else in all creation, will be able to separate us from the love of God that is in Christ Jesus our Lord. (Rom. 8:38–39)

Affirmation: Nothing will cause God to abandon his love for me.

Radar: This week I am seeing the following patterns in my relationships that I need to change to recover from dependency:

Action Step: This week if I hear another person make a disparaging comment about me, I will not join in, laugh, or agree with the comment.

- The comment:
- The person who made the comment:
- What happened when I failed to join in:

Gratitude List

The positive things I am learning this week about myself:

1.

2.

3.

The positive things I am learning this week about others:

1.

2.

3.

The positive things I am learning this week about God:

1.

2.

3.

Week 3

Prayer

Father God, so often I listen to other voices tell me what is right and true about myself, about others, and about you. This week may I listen for your voice, for your truth, for your Word. When there is a difference in the voices, help me to listen only to yours.

Word of Truth

There is no fear in love. But perfect love drives out fear, because fear has to do with punishment. The one who fears is not made perfect in love. (1 John 4:18)

Affirmation: God's perfect love for me is able to help me overcome my fears.

Radar: This week I am seeing the following patterns in my relationships that I need to change to recover from dependency:

Action Step: This week when I hear the voice of fear speaking lies into my life, I will turn up the volume, listen to the lies, and denounce them in the name of Jesus.

- The lies:
- As far as I can remember, when I first believed the lies:
- The truth I am learning that I will use to denounce the lies:

Gratitude List

The positive things I am learning this week about myself:

1.

2.

3.

The positive things I am learning this week about others:

1.

2.

3.

The positive things I am learning this week about God:

1.

2.

3.

Week 4

Prayer

God in heaven, you show great patience with me. You know I am not perfect. You show me grace and allow me time to grow. I need to learn to be patient with myself. Help me to trust that because you are patient with me, I can be patient with myself.

Word of Truth

The Lord is not slow in keeping his promise, as some understand slowness. Instead he is patient with you, not wanting anyone to perish, but everyone to come to repentance. (2 Pet. 3:9)

Affirmation: Because God is patient with me, I can be patient with myself.

Radar: This week I am seeing the following patterns in my relationships that I need to change to recover from dependency:

Action Step: This week when I become impatient with myself, I will take a deep breath and remember this week's affirmation.

- What I became impatient about:
- Why I became impatient:
- How I felt when I gave myself grace:

Gratitude List

The positive things I am learning this week about myself:

1.

2.

3.

The positive things I am learning this week about others:

1.

2.

3.

The positive things I am learning this week about God:

1.

2.

3.

Week 5

Prayer

I have so often tried to change and have failed, Lord. Help me to realize my failures were because I was trying to change on my own. I need your help to change. I need your help to know I can change. Lord, change me.

Word of Truth

Love does not delight in evil but rejoices with the truth. It always protects, always trusts, always hopes, always perseveres. (1 Cor. 13:6–7)

Affirmation: God's love perseveres for me so I can persevere for good and for God.

Radar: This week I am seeing the following patterns in my relationships that I need to change to recover from dependency:

Action Step: This week I will identify one small change I need to make in how I relate to others and will commit to making that change.

- The change:
- Why I need to make this change:
- How I will make this change:

Gratitude List

The positive things I am learning this week about myself:

1.

2.

3.

The positive things I am learning this week about others:

1.

2.

3.

The positive things I am learning this week about God:

1.

2.

3.

Week 6

Prayer

Dear God, there are people in my life who will not understand the changes I need to make. Help me to be brave and make those changes, even in the face of opposition. When I am ridiculed or opposed, help me to look to you for strength, guidance, and security.

Word of Truth

Be strong and courageous. Do not be afraid or terrified because of them, for the LORD your God goes with you; he will never leave you nor forsake you. (Deut. 31:6)

Affirmation: I can be brave because God will never leave me or forsake me.

Radar: This week I am seeing the following patterns in my relationships that I need to change to recover from dependency:

Action Step: This week I will do one thing I am afraid of.

- The one thing I did:
- Why I have always been afraid:
- How I felt after I did the one thing:

Gratitude List

The positive things I am learning this week about myself:

1.

2.

3.

The positive things I am learning this week about others:

1.

2.

3.

The positive things I am learning this week about God:

1.

2.

3.

Week 7

Prayer

Father God, I struggle with the fear that I am not enough. I struggle with the fear that I will fail. Help me to overcome my fear, to put my faith in what you can do through me. Help me to focus on you for my success.

Word of Truth

I can do all this through him who gives me strength. (Phil. 4:13)

Affirmation: My strength for change comes from God.

Radar: This week I am seeing the following patterns in my relationships that I need to change to recover from dependency:

Action Step: This week I will identify a fear I've been unwilling to change, and I will commit to praying about this fear each day.

- The fear:
- When I first felt the fear:
- Why I have not given up this fear before now:

Gratitude List

The positive things I am learning this week about myself:

1.

2.

3.

The positive things I am learning this week about others:

1.

2.

3.

The positive things I am learning this week about God:

1.

2.

3.

Week 8

Prayer

I confess, Father, I have become comfortable with my fears. I am afraid to leave their pit. I confess I have spent more time getting used to my pit than I have spent with you. Give me courage to walk away from the pit and toward you.

Word of Truth

> He lifted me out of the slimy pit,
>   out of the mud and mire;
> he set my feet on a rock
>   and gave me a firm place to stand. (Ps. 40:2)

Affirmation: God can lift me out of this pit of dependency and give me a firm place to stand.

Radar: This week I am seeing the following patterns in my relationships that I need to change to recover from dependency:

Action Step: This week I will:

- draw a picture of the pit I have allowed myself to stay in.
- label all aspects of my pit, including the people who occupy my pit with me.
- identify at least three actions I am taking to climb up out of the pit.

Gratitude List

The positive things I am learning this week about myself:

1.

2.

3.

The positive things I am learning this week about others:

1.

2.

3.

The positive things I am learning this week about God:

1.

2.

3.

Week 9

Prayer

God, you call me your child. Jesus, you call me your friend. These are relationships I have trouble understanding and believing in. I confess I sought instead the approval and affirmation of others. Help me to choose relationships that support my relationship with you.

Word of Truth

I no longer call you servants, because a servant does not know his master's business. Instead, I have called you friends, for everything that I learned from my Father I have made known to you. (John 15:15)

Affirmation: I am both child and friend of the Creator of the world.

Radar: This week I am seeing the following patterns in my relationships that I need to change to recover from dependency:

Action Step: This week I will spend time specifically in fellowship with my Father and Friend. I will find a way to spend that time away from any other distraction so I can focus on God and Christ.

- When I spent time with God and Christ:
- How I spent time with God and Christ:
- What I learned from spending time with God and Christ:

Gratitude List

The positive things I am learning this week about myself:

1.

2.

3.

The positive things I am learning this week about others:

1.

2.

3.

The positive things I am learning this week about God:

1.

2.

3.

Week 10

Prayer

I know you love me, Lord, but I have trouble loving myself. When I see myself, I see all the mistakes I've made. I do not feel worthy of your love. I feel so unworthy of your love that I have difficulty believing your love is real. This week, Lord, help me to feel and know your love.

Word of Truth

> For you created my inmost being;
>   you knit me together in my mother's womb.
> I praise you because I am fearfully and wonderfully
>   made;
>   your works are wonderful,
>   I know that full well. (Ps. 139:13–14)

Affirmation: I am a wonderful work of God.

Radar: This week I am seeing the following patterns in my relationships that I need to change to recover from dependency:

Action Step: This week I will do something nice for myself, something involving only myself, something I have wanted to do for myself but have been unwilling to do.

- What I did for myself:
- Why I have been unwilling in the past to do this for myself:
- How I felt doing something nice for me alone:

Gratitude List

The positive things I am learning this week about myself:

1.

2.

3.

The positive things I am learning this week about others:

1.

2.

3.

The positive things I am learning this week about God:

1.

2.

3.

Week 11

Prayer

Change can be so difficult, Father, but I want to change the way I feel and relate to myself, to others, and to you. On my own, I fear I don't have the strength to maintain positive changes. I am afraid I will go back to the way I was. Help me to know that when my strength and courage come from you, I cannot fail because you cannot fail.

Word of Truth

Be on your guard; stand firm in the faith; be courageous; be strong. (1 Cor. 16:13)

Affirmation: God is able to strengthen me with faith and courage.

Radar: This week I am seeing the following patterns in my relationships that I need to change to recover from dependency:

Action Step: This week I commit to using the strength and faith God gives me to forgive myself for the wrongs I have done to myself.

- The wrong I forgave:
- The strength and courage I gained from God:
- The freedom I've found from that strength, courage, and forgiveness:

Gratitude List

The positive things I am learning this week about myself:

1.

2.

3.

The positive things I am learning this week about others:

1.

2.

3.

The positive things I am learning this week about God:

1.

2.

3.

Week 12

Prayer

You are my faithful God and Father. I praise you for the strength and courage to accomplish changes over these past weeks. Lord, I thank you for what you have done. I thank you for what you will do. I know that your power is mighty and your love is great! Sustain me in that knowledge as I continue my journey of recovery.

Word of Truth

Do not conform to the pattern of this world, but be transformed by the renewing of your mind. Then you will be able to test and approve what God's will is—his good, pleasing and perfect will. (Rom. 12:2)

Affirmation: I do not need to conform to the past because God is able to transform my future.

Radar: This week I am seeing the following patterns in my relationships that I need to change to recover from dependency:

Action Step: This week I will choose an object of the past twelve weeks of transformation to help me remember all that God has done for me and has yet to do in me.

- The object I chose:
- Why I chose this object:
- What the object says to me:

Gratitude List

The positive things I am learning this week about myself:

1.

2.

3.

The positive things I am learning this week about others:

1.

2.

3.

The positive things I am learning this week about God:

1.

2.

3.

We are so grateful for the opportunity to share, in this small way, your vital and courageous journey to recovery from relationship dependency. We encourage you to continue to grow, to learn, and to know and fight for the truth. And what is the truth? The truth is that God deeply, passionately loves you and desires for your relationships to reflect his heart, his character, and his love. Please don't settle for less.

May God continue to show you that he "is able to do immeasurably more than all [you] ask or imagine, according to his power that is at work within [you]" (Eph. 3:20). We are confident "that he who began a good work in you will carry it on to completion" (Phil. 1:6).

Notes

Chapter 3: What Are the Patterns of Relationship Dependency?

1. http://www.merriam-webster.com/dictionary/honeymoon.

Chapter 5: How Does Emotional Abuse Contribute to Relationship Dependency?

1. http://www.brainyquote.com/quotes/quotes/b/briangreen551482.html.

2. Please see the information provided on overprotective and overindulgent parents in Dr. Tim Clinton and Gary Sibcy, *Loving Your Child Too Much* (Nashville: Thomas Nelson, 2012). Those traits include viewing children as fragile or as possessions instead of as a gift, allowing no opportunity or consequences for mistakes, and avoiding unpleasant feelings. See their helpful chart here: http://books.google.com/books?id=1p8rH3ml2gwC&pg=PA214&source=gbs_selected_pages&cad=3#v=onepage&q&f=false.

Chapter 7: What Is the Role of the Brain in Relationship Dependency?

1. http://www.huffingtonpost.com/2012/02/13/falling-in-love-triggers-brain-changes_n_1273196.html.

2. Ibid.

3. http://www.ncbi.nlm.nih.gov/pubmed/22885871.

4. http://www.science20.com/news_articles/link_between_dopamine_and_expectation_pleasure_confirmed.

5. http://www.medicineonline.com/news/10/5323/Problem-Gamblers-Show-Brain-Impairment.html.

6. http://www.science20.com/news_releases/anxiety_disorders_the_dop amine_connection_and_why_it_actually_is_all_in_your_head.

Chapter 8: What Is the Role of Attachment Styles in Relationship Dependency?

1. Tim Clinton and Gary Sibcy, *Why You Do the Things You Do: The Secret to Healthy Relationships* (Nashville: Thomas Nelson, 2006), 23.

Chapter 10: How Do You Start Relationship Recovery?

1. http://www.goodreads.com/quotes/264407-faith-is-like-radar-that-sees -through-the-fog---.

Dr. Gregory L. Jantz, PhD, is a popular speaker and award-winning author of more than twenty-five books, including *Healing the Scars of Emotional Abuse* and *Every Woman's Guide to Managing Your Anger*. He is the founder of the Center for Counseling and Health Resources, Inc. (www. aplaceofhope.com) in the state of Washington.

Tim Clinton, EdD, is president of the nearly fifty-thousand-member American Association of Christian Counselors (AACC), the largest and most diverse Christian counseling association in the world. He is professor of counseling and pastoral care and executive director of the Center for Counseling and Family Studies at Liberty University. He is recognized as a world leader in faith and mental health issues and has authored over twenty books including *Breakthrough: When to Give In, When to Push Back.*

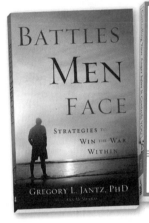

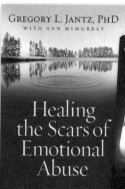
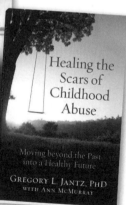